Modern Peacemakers

Kofi
Annan

Guiding the United Nations

MODERN PEACEMAKERS

Modern Peacemakers

Kofi Annan

Guiding the United Nations

Rachel A. Koestler-Grack

CHELSEA HOUSE
PUBLISHERS
An imprint of Infobase Publishing

Kofi Annan

Chelsea House
An imprint of Infobase Publishing
132 West 31st Street
New York NY 10001

ISBN-10: 0-7910-8996-7
ISBN-13: 978-0-7910-8996-5

Library of Congress Cataloging-in-Publication Data

Koestler-Grack, Rachel A., 1973–
  Kofi Annan : guiding the United Nations / Rachel A. Koestler-Grack.
    p. cm. — (Modern peacemakers)
  Includes bibliographical references and index.
  ISBN 0-7910-8996-7
  1. Annan, Kofi A. (Kofi Atta) 2. United Nations—Biography. 3. Statesmen—Ghana—Biography. 4. World politics—1989– I. Title. II. Title.
    D839.7.A56K64 2006
    341.23092—dc22   2006020450

TABLE OF CONTENTS

CHAPTER 1

Not Afraid
to Dream

Just before midnight in East Timor on May 20, 2002, United Nations (UN) Secretary-General Kofi Annan stood center stage under blinding spotlights. The sound of violins, flutes, tambourines, and hundreds of singing voices filled the air with excitement and energy. Children, some in white dresses carrying candles, others holding red, yellow, and blue fish kites on poles, paraded through the crowd. As Annan started to speak, a hush swept over the audience. "I hearby declare East Timor an independent democratic republic, dedicated to the rule of law and the rights of man," he said with a sturdy voice. "Long live East Timor."[1]

The crowd burst into shouts and cheers. As East Timorese citizens slowly raised their new flag up the pole, fireworks exploded in the black sky. Annan never thought he would get to see two countries gain their independence in his lifetime. The first time was his home country of Ghana, when Annan was a teenager. Forty years later, he stood thousands of miles from his homeland, handing over freedom to the East Timorese. The people of this tiny island—located between the Indian Ocean and the South China Sea—had clawed their way

East Timor's incoming president, Xanana Gusmao (right), embraces United Nations Secretary-General Kofi Annan during East Timor's independence celebration on May 20, 2002. The tiny nation declared independence after 24 years of oppression under rule by Indonesia, which had followed centuries of Portuguese colonization.

back from catastrophe to become an independent nation in a little more than a year. They did not fight alone, however, and for Annan, it had been a long and tiring road.

THE ROAD TO INDEPENDENCE

In August 1999, after 24 years of brutal and oppressive rule by Indonesia, a popular referendum on the status of the state was sponsored by the United Nations. The East Timorese voted for freedom. An Indonesian-backed militia retaliated with a bloodbath of massacre, rape, and looting. The militia bullied its way across East Timor, street by street, village by village, setting every house ablaze. A small country about which no one cared before, East Timor suddenly became a hot topic to Annan. He knew that if the international community did not intervene, the destruction would continue and the loss of life would be horrific. At the same time, he knew that no UN member state would be willing to march into East Timor without the consent of Indonesia.

Annan spent countless hours trying to convince the Indonesian president that the people of East Timor needed help, but that the international community did not want to come in to protect the lives on this island and encounter a confrontation. Dedicated and determined, Annan made trip after trip to Indonesia, some nights sleeping only two or three hours. With unshakeable resolve, he pushed through the Security Council and had peacekeeping troops deployed to East Timor. When the Indonesian military finally withdrew, all that remained were the smoldering shells of buildings and homes—no roofs, no windows—and the tears of the survivors.

In February 2000, hundreds of United Nations peacekeepers began working with the East Timorese to rebuild their nation. In the months that followed, the United Nations was responsible for everything a government would normally be responsible for, such as ensuring that clinics and hospitals were running and schools opened. After watching his own country struggle through independence, Annan understood the daunting task that lay ahead for the East Timorese. Even though they had pulled together as a nation and fought for and won their independence, the hardest part lay ahead: building a freestanding country. Annan pledged the UN's help along the way.

"We should see our role as builders," Annan explained. "When you're building a house, you put the scaffolding around it, and you continue construction. When the construction is done, you peel off and remove the scaffolding. But the building stands. And that is the role the UN would want to see here."[2] Remembering his teenage years, Annan was exhilarated a year later, when

Above, hundreds of East Timorese children hold candles during the country's 2002 independence celebration. Under Secretary-General Annan, the United Nations placed peacekeeping forces in East Timor in 2000 to begin the process of building an independent nation.

he officially passed the power over to East Timor, a free and independent nation.

As Annan boarded a plane back to New York, he probably smiled to himself, recalling the laughter of a Timorese boy. He knew he had played a part in that child's happiness. Few people believed independence was possible for this speck of a country. The fire must have ignited in someone's heart, though; perhaps many years ago, a single boy had visions of peace and freedom. Annan could relate to this situation. He explained,

> Sometimes I suggest we do things, and people say, "Mr. Secretary, this is a dream, you are a dreamer." I say, "I'm not afraid to dream. You first have to start with a dream. Build your castles

in the sky, and give them foundation. Without a dream, you are not going to get anywhere."[3]

Of course, not all UN missions have a happy ending. Annan and the thousands of other civil service workers at the United Nations dedicate every day of their lives to trying to make the world a better place for humanity. They find ways to make peace, keep people safe and healthy, and bring basic needs to those living in poverty. Sadly, these are jobs that will never come to an end. On the day Kofi Annan stood before thousands of East Timorese, declaring them independent, there were 24 major armed conflicts waging throughout the world. Thirteen million refugees could not return home, 40 million people were living with HIV or AIDS, and half of the people in the world were existing on less than two dollars a day. No doubt, Annan's smile on his plane ride home lasted only a moment. The secretary-general had so much more to do.

CHAPTER 2

Growing Pains

On April 8, 1938, Kofi Atta Annan was born in Kumasi, an inland city of present-day Ghana. In Ghana, a boy born on a Friday was traditionally named "Kofi." At the time of Kofi's birth, Ghana was a British-ruled colony known as the Gold Coast. It lies in the shoulder of West Africa, bordering the Gulf of Guinea, an inlet of the Atlantic Ocean. As a child, Kofi would have walked beneath the thick, green canopy of rain forest trees. He and his twin sister, Efua, probably watched farmers pick limes, bananas, yams, and cacao. Kofi's parents—Henry and Victoria—were descendants of Fanti chiefs. The Fanti people are an ethnic group of West Africa. Originally, the Fanti lived along the west coast of Africa. But more than 300 years ago, they began to move inland, finally ending up in and around Kumasi.

Henry Annan was a quiet and thoughtful man, who followed his ancestors—a long line of chiefs—as a Fanti nobleman and an elected governor of the Ashanti province. In Ghana, the role of chiefs is to listen, to judge, to provide leadership, and to end disputes. From a very early age, Kofi watched his father perform these tasks, gaining a

Portuguese, Dutch, and English traders had an important base in the coastal town of Elmina, Ghana, pictured above. Kofi Annan was born in Kumasi, an inland city in Ghana, which was then known as the Gold Coast.

wisdom he would use often later in life. Growing up in Ghana, Kofi always had someone to go to in order to seek advice—uncles, cousins, aunts, and grandmothers. Often, they used proverbs to teach. Once, during an interview, Kofi gave an example: He could have gone to his father and said he was angry at his boss. Kofi would say, "I'm going to go to the office tomorrow and tell him off." Henry would calmly reply, "Son, sit down and look at me. You don't hit a man on the head if you've got your fingers between his teeth."[4] That would be all, and Kofi would have to walk away and figure it out.

THE ASHANTI PEOPLE

In the 1700s, the great king Osei Tutu founded the Ashanti kingdom. One of his priests, Komfo Anokye, unified the Ashanti states through an allegiance to the Golden Stool—a chair that, according to Ashanti tradition, miraculously descended from the heavens. Komfo planted two trees in the forest and predicted that one tree would live to become the capital of Ashanti. Therefore, the Ashanti people named their capital *Kumasi,* meaning "the tree lived." The place where Komfo planted the other tree was called *Kumawa*—"the tree died."

When Europeans began arriving in the area, the Ashanti people waged vigorous wars against the British, who built forts and castles to the south of Kumasi. In early years, the Fanti and the Ashanti were enemies. In 1844, the Fanti and other tribes signed a treaty with the British, placing their part of the Gold Coast under Britain's protection. The powerful Ashanti resented this bond between the Fanti and the British. They believed the Fanti were betraying their homeland and African heritage. Fighting erupted between the Ashanti and the British in 1873. The British captured Kumasi but failed to snatch the sacred Golden Stool. With the Golden Stool still in their hands, the Ashanti believed they could eventually defeat the British Army.

In 1901, the Ashanti led a final uprising against the British. This war ended with the Ashanti nation's bitter defeat. After the war, the British united the Ashanti region with neighboring territories and formed the Gold Coast Colony.

A TROUBLED PAST

In order to understand Kofi Annan's childhood, it is important to know the history of Africa. Kofi was born into a world of

Ashanti King Otumfuo Opoku Ware II sits with his court in Kumasi in this 1995 photograph. The legendary Golden Stool (on the right) is a symbol of Ashanti power. During a battle with the British in 1873, the British captured the city of Kumasi, but not the Golden Stool; therefore, the Ashanti believed they could still defeat the colonists.

instability, turbulence, and change. At the time of his birth, his home country of Ghana was on the verge of becoming independent, throwing off the yoke of hundreds of years under colonial rule. Developing a new nation meant many growing pains and an intense fight for freedom, but Kofi's people were ready to do whatever it took to gain independence.

Africa is the world's second largest continent. The United States could fit inside it more than three times. Africa's mammoth size makes it a place of tremendous diversity, holding between its coastlines some 54 countries. It is home to a wide variety of peoples, languages, and cultures. Today, the people of many cultures across Africa speak more than 1,000 different languages. The equator slices Africa almost exactly in half, making it the most tropical continent in the world. Nevertheless, Africa's climate is amazingly diverse. The continent is home to broad-shouldered plateaus; snow-tipped mountains; lush rain forests, wide, barren deserts, and breathtaking rivers and lakes. Africa boasts the longest river, the Nile, and the largest desert, the stretching sands of the Sahara.

Africa has sometimes been called the "Cradle of Humanity" because many of the oldest human fossils were found there. It is the site of the world's earliest known civilization—that of the Egyptians, who flourished in the Nile valley thousands of years ago. African kingdoms of fabulous wealth and rich culture existed long before European empires ever came into being. The continent's vast differences in rainfall, soil richness, and plant and animal life tested the survival skills of early Africans. Over thousands of years, these cultures struggled through continual adjustment and hard work.

About 500 years before Kofi was born, Africans were introduced to a new challenge that would change their homeland forever—the arrival of European sailors. In 1471, Portuguese sailors landed in present-day Ghana. They gazed, wide-eyed, at the abundance of gold the Africans had to trade. There was so much gold in the region that Europeans began calling it the "Gold Coast." Before long, European countries started competing with each other over trading rights for the riches of Africa. They built forts along the coast. Little did the natives know, however, that it was only a matter of time before Europeans would establish permanent settlements on the continent and claim the land as their own.

At first, Europeans were only interested in trading gold, spices, and ivory. Before long, though, they discovered a new market— African slaves. At this time, most Europeans believed whites were superior to Africans. They saw the natives as savages, incapable of creating powerful civilizations, having great ideas, or taking care of themselves. Europeans were terribly wrong, however. Perhaps

Africans lacked the technology of Europeans, but they were far from simple-minded. Over thousands of years, Africans had sustained powerful empires and built mind-boggling temples and cities.

European slave traders were narrow-minded and ignorant of other cultures, however. They kidnapped countless men, women, and children. They snatched Africans from their villages and homeland, forced them on to filthy ships, and sent them across the Atlantic Ocean to the Americas. In America, Africans were sold as slaves to rich colonists and plantation owners. For 300 years, many Africans suffered this painful and devastating fate.

In the early 1500s, the powerful Ashanti defeated their African rivals in the Gold Coast. They captured many prisoners and marched them to the coast to be sold to the highest European bidder. Often, they exchanged their African captives for rum, cloth, and beads. The Gold Coast soon became a huge market for African slaves.

Slavery was a common practice in African wars. Captors often sold their prisoners as slaves to other African peoples. In Africa, however, slaves were usually treated well. This was not the case with European buyers. One in every eight of the millions of Africans who sailed to America died during the ocean voyage. Also, unlike slaves in Africa, captives sent to America had little chance of ever regaining their freedom.

Africans who remained in their homeland did not fare much better. European powers such as Britain, France, Germany, Portugal, and Spain divided up the continent into many colonies. African communities were often split down the middle and forced to join neighboring groups. New European governments moved in to replace native rulers. Sometimes, local chiefs served as advisors or go-betweens to the people, but more often, European rulers forced them to step down completely. All across the continent, African people were oppressed. The new governments passed laws stating that Africans could not own land. Countless natives lost farms and other property that had been theirs for generations. Suddenly, independent workers had no choice but to go to work for Europeans. Day in and day out, they performed grueling labor in horrible conditions and for low wages.

Europeans cared little about building up Africa. They pumped the country of its resources and riches, which they then shipped off to their home countries. While Europe's wealth piled higher, the heavy hand of poverty pressed down on African villages. No doubt young Kofi heard the stories of his country's troubled past many times. He probably listened in puzzlement, wondering how a proud and powerful people could suffer such terrible misfortune.

AFRICA FIGHTS BACK

The people of Africa did not just stand around while Europeans ran over their continent. At first, Africans fought their invad-

Volta-Bani Uprising

During the early 1900s, natives grew restless in the western Volta region of what was then French West Africa—which primarily included much of present-day Mali and Burkina Faso. In the final months of 1915, leaders of 11 villages gathered around a shrine and took an oath of war. They pledged rebellion against the colonial government. Thus began one of the last and bloodiest wars of colonial West Africa—the Volta-Bani uprising.

Anticolonial leaders did not march into this dangerous fight or blindly lash out in a sudden fit of rage. Their revolt was calculated. They were well-armed, trained warriors, who had tremendous confidence in their gods. As the war waged, people of the Volta-Bani quickly proved their genius for military strategies and tactics. With World War I raging in Europe, the colonial military presence in West Africa had been reduced substantially. With keen eyes, natives watched the colonial forces plucked away—soldier by soldier—to fight the war back home. They knew the colonial government would have little chance of crushing a rebellion, and they chose this time to strike.

ers, but their weapons were no match for the modern machines and warfare of the Europeans. Uprisings were quickly squashed, and Africans had little choice but to try to make the best of their new lives.

Some African traders still made a modest living by running small businesses. In some areas, educated Africans eventually managed to secure positions in the European-dominated government. These instances were few and far between, however. Most Africans were too poor and powerless to become part of the "better class." Their only choice was a hard one: Give in or revolt.

Many natives responded by revolting. Instead of fighting to keep invaders out of Africa, they protested new hardships. They lashed out against forced labor, forfeited lands, colonial taxes, and much more. Some protests were peaceful, but others turned violent. Often, the uprisings were small, lost in the jungles and barely

The war took place in four separate arenas, involving more than 800,000 Africans from 1,000 villages. At times, the African side unleashed armies of 15,000 to 20,000, making it the largest resistance to colonialism in Africa. In February 1916, the French army began a strike-back campaign of repression. Soldiers swept the countryside, destroying anything and everything in their path. Within one short month, the army had depleted its ammunition supplies, however, and had to return to the headquarters to restock. The rebels saw this move as a retreat, and the apparent victory fueled the resistance. More villages picked up arms and joined the fight for freedom. The resistance continued to spread through the region. As the French crushed one rebellion, another ferocious battle would arise somewhere else.

In 1917, the Africans were ultimately defeated by superior French firepower, and the leaders of the uprising were put to death. There was no treaty, however—no peace agreement between the natives and the colonial regime. Each village surrendered separately and offered no collective defeat. For years afterward, the French feared that the violent uprisings would begin again.

noticed by European governments. To many Africans, it seemed as though their situation would never improve.

As the years stretched on, Africans turned their attention from small revolts to bigger dreams. They heard of other countries around the world fighting for independence. Perhaps the key to winning freedom from their oppressors was to unite as one country. This belief gave birth to nationalism—the idea that people of different backgrounds living in a colony could become free if they joined together as a nation. This system had worked for the Europeans in America, Italy, and other countries around the world. Many Africans believed it could liberate them, too.

In March 1920, 45 West Africans—members of the educated elite—gathered in the Gold Coast. There, they founded the National Congress of British West Africa (NCBWA). Representatives came from each of the four West African colonies—Nigeria, the Gold Coast, Sierra Leone, and the Gambia. At this first conference, the NCBWA pushed for "a united West Africa." They pressed the British government to let them join the colonial parliaments. Members hoped they could make changes from within the current European government. The British denied all the NCBWA's demands, however. The primary weakness of the NCBWA was that its members were all from the privileged upper class, and they refused to call on the common people for support.

At this time, people in East and Central Africa spoke little or nothing of nationalism. In these places, the educated elite barely existed yet. The ideas of nationalism and independence developed at different rates across the wide African continent. European colonists from coast to coast assumed that they would dominate the future of these countries indefinitely.

GHANA GAINS INDEPENDENCE

Young Kofi Annan's life began in surroundings marred by pain, tragedy, and fighting. From a very early age, he faced the realities of war. He probably heard daily news of protests, revolts, or injustices. These experiences no doubt in-spired Kofi to dream about a world where people from different cultures respected one another and lived in peace.

When Kofi was nine years old, another anticolonial group met in the Gold Coast. The United Gold Coast Convention (UGCC) was formed in 1947. Their goal was to put pressure on the British government to grant independence to the Gold Coast colony. Again, the UGCC hoped to move carefully and quietly—without enlisting mass support. Things turned out much differently than they had planned, however.

The UGCC hired Kwame Nkrumah as their secretary. Nkrumah had just arrived home from several years of college in the United States. Eager to join the UGCC, Nkrumah immediately went to work. His ideas of liberation took a different road than the rest of the group, though. Nkrumah believed that action by the masses was the only way to get results, and he began to organize. He found that many young nationalists were on his side. These activists called for a country-wide campaign against the British government. Soon, Nkrumah organized strikes and boycotts of imported goods.

At this point, the UGCC leaders began to regret their choice of Nkrumah as secretary, but it was too late. A tidal wave of mass protest swept across British West Africa. The protests and demonstrations shattered the Gold Coast government. For years, the British viewed the Gold Coast as a model colony—always peaceful and patient. Suddenly, it exploded into a battleground of riots and chaos. Just down the road from the castle, in the middle of Accra, angry crowds looted and burned European shops. The rioting spread to neighboring towns. Many people died and numerous properties were destroyed before the police and army could restore order.

The British governor arrested six key leaders of the UGCC, including Nkrumah. Although Nkrumah encouraged mass support, he had nothing to do with the riots. The police wanted to prove that the UGCC was part of a Communist plot against the

The Duchess of Kent, seated center on dais, reads a message from the Queen of England in the parliament house in Accra, Ghana, in this 1957 photograph. That same year, Ghana was the first colony south of the Sahara to gain its independence from colonial rule.

government, but all six leaders had to be released for lack of evidence. After their unpleasant jail experience, the other five leaders were determined to get rid of Nkrumah, whom they blamed for the trouble. The UGCC accepted the warning and was ready to go slowly, but Nkrumah had other ideas.

Dismissed by the UGCC, Nkrumah and his followers formed their own group, the Convention People's Party (CPP), in June 1949. The party was ready to use mass support to win independence. On January 8, 1950, the party began a strike through the trade unions. The governor—still annoyed by earlier riots—

answered their peaceful protest with violence. Arrests turned into fighting, and two policemen were killed in the clashes. On January 21, police arrested Nkrumah.

With Nkrumah in prison, the colony grew increasingly restless. The British decided to change their stand. Under pressure from the masses, they agreed to hold a new general election. This action would ultimately lead to a constitution and make the first steps toward independence.

In February 1951, CPP candidates won a sweeping victory. Although he was still in prison, Nkrumah won almost all the votes in Accra. The newly appointed British governor, Sir Charles Arden-Clarke, at once commented, "Nkrumah and his party had the mass of the people behind them."[5] He released Nkrumah from jail and appointed him leader of an African parliament, which would give Africans some degree of self-government. The governor promised independence would come later.

People in the Gold Coast struggled for independence for another six years. Finally, in 1957, the Gold Coast became the independent nation of Ghana. Ghana was the first colony south of the Sahara Desert to gain independence. Ghana proved that no matter how tough and tall the barriers to freedom rose, they could be overcome. Africans could successfully endure the growing pains toward independence. One by one, colonial governments began crumbling like sand castles across Africa. Ghana had a special place in African consciousness. It was at the center of African imagination. These people paved the road for the independence movement.

Kofi was 19 years old when Ghana gained its independence. "As a teenager, we didn't stop talking politics at school," he remembered, "because it would only involve flaying the struggle for independence. And we saw the whole nation demanding and fighting for independence and wanting to take charge of his own destiny. It was electrifying."[6] He, too, played an active role in achieving freedom and justice—even as a youngster.

CHAPTER 3

Young Leader

Throughout much of the 1950s, Kofi Annan followed the events of Africa's fight for independence from the safety of a boarding school and later from the University of Science and Technology in his hometown of Kumasi. He was too young to join the military, but Kofi found other ways to fight for justice. In many ways, the changing world around him shaped Kofi into a young man of drive and conviction. On one occasion, he led his fellow classmates in a hunger strike to demand better food—and won. Even at an early age, his leadership abilities were beginning to develop.

As a teenager and young man, Kofi stood in the midst of an amazing revolution. He later recalled:

I saw lots of change taking place around me—and major changes, where the colonial power was handing over the country to what we called then "freedom fighters," where people like Nkrumah and others came from jail and became prime ministers and presidents. And so [I grew] up believing that change is possible. That all is possible, and that one can dare to make a difference, one can dare change.[7]

While attending the University of Science and Technology, Kofi developed a keen vision for the complicated world around him. But he still had much to learn. One day, the headmaster walked into one of Kofi's classrooms. He set up a wide piece of white paper. In the center of the sheet was a black dot. "Boys, what do you see?" the headmaster asked.

"A black dot!" the students shouted in unison.

The headmaster narrowed his eyes in disappointment. "So not a single one of you saw the broad white sheet of paper? Don't go through life with that attitude."[8] This lesson was one Kofi would never forget. In fact, he would soon get to put this skill of "seeing the big picture" to the test.

HALFWAY AROUND THE WORLD

During the 1958–1959 school year, 20-year-old Kofi Annan served as vice president of the national student union, an organization made up of students from all over Ghana. At a meeting in Sierra Leone, Kofi met a talent scout from the Ford Foundation. Founded in 1936 with donations from automakers Henry and Edsel Ford, this charitable organization promotes peace efforts, human welfare, and environmental protection. At that time, the foundation held a Foreign Students Leadership Project, in which students could win a scholarship to a university in the United States. Kofi's eloquence and commanding leadership impressed the scout, and he won the scholarship. Kofi's achievement sent him on a new and exciting adventure in a much broader context, halfway around the world.

Before beginning his first school year, Kofi attended a summer program at Harvard University in Cambridge, Massachusetts. There he learned that teaching methods in the United States were quite different from those back in Kumasi. He was probably relieved that he had the summer to adjust to this new culture. In late summer, Kofi boarded a plane for the midwestern United States. He would begin his U.S. college experience at Macalester College in St. Paul, Minnesota.

In Minnesota, Kofi learned that more things, besides classrooms, differed from Africa. The weather turned out to be a shock. Of course, Kofi had read about the seasons, and he thought he knew all about Minnesota winters. In tropical Africa, Kofi was used to two seasons—wet and dry. Although he quickly tired of donning layers of clothing just to go outside, he assumed that would be enough. The one winter accessory he refused to wear was earmuffs. "I thought they were inelegant and ugly,"[9] Kofi commented. One day, he went out to get something to eat, and the freezing winds nipped so fiercely at his ears, he thought they would freeze and fall off. "I went out and bought the biggest pair I could find the next day,"[10] Kofi remembered. Kofi learned more from that incident than how to avoid frostbitten ears, however. He decided, "You don't walk into any situation and pretend you know better than the natives."[11] This lesson has stayed with him every day since.

At Macalester College, Kofi also learned about the importance of world peace and international relationships. The United Nations flag flew alongside the U.S. flag on all Macalester flagpoles. Part of the faculty's mission was to teach students to be good world citizens. Peace was at the forefront. "Macalester's academic excellence is deeply rooted in a reverence and respect for other cultures," Kofi remembered. "The focus which I found here has never failed me."[12]

Once he became accustomed to the seasons, Kofi quickly fell into place in Minnesota. Being a track star at the University of Science and Technology in Kumasi, he naturally joined the track team. In the 1960 Minnesota state championships, his team took first place. He even set a school record in the 60-yard dash. His fearless nature prompted him to try out for football—a sport he had never played in Ghana. "I was OK as long as I kept running and no one caught up with me," he joked about his first football practice. "Otherwise, I was like a piece of paper—I weighed 138 pounds, and that's not football weight. So I gave it up after fifteen minutes."[13] Instead, he decided to join the soccer team.

Kofi also succeeded academically. He was a state champion orator, a member of the debate team, and he served as president of the Cosmopolitan Club—a group that encouraged friendship between American and international students. As his college years passed by, it became more and more apparent that Annan had a gift for public relations. In 1960, Harry Morgan, head of Macalester's International Center, picked Annan and three other students to travel across the country as part of a program to take foreign students on the road to see America. While rumbling along in their donated Rambler station wagon, they hoped to "catch America off-guard whenever possible."[14] The group—who called themselves the Ambassadors of Friendship—would stop at random places along the way and ask for some spontaneous hospitality. Kofi still recalls an evening they spent at the Salvation Army home for the poor in Kansas. They even spent one night in a jail in Flagstaff, Arizona—as guests of the local sheriff.

REMINDERS OF HOME

Even though America was quite different from Africa, Kofi encountered some striking reminders of home. During the 1960s, African Americans were engaged in their own struggle for justice. At that time, African Americans were not treated as equal to whites. Many public places were segregated. Throughout the South and in some parts of the North, city officials forced African Americans to use separate bathrooms, restaurants, movie theaters, shops, and even drinking fountains. For years, most African Americans in the South attended separate schools, which lacked supplies and adequate teachers, and were often rundown. African Americans could use only the back seats of public buses and had to sit in separate waiting rooms at bus and train stations. Laws even forbade African Americans from voting.

Finally, this unequal treatment erupted in protests and demonstrations across the country—especially in the South. This period of history became known as the civil rights movement. Civil rights activists participated in marches, sit-ins, voter registration drives, and boycotts, hoping to end segregation and change racial laws. After the U.S. government outlawed segregation on public transportation in 1961, activists organized "Freedom Rides" in the eastern United States. Freedom Riders rode buses from state to state on integrated buses, hoping to enforce this new law.

As in Africa, many whites disagreed with desegregation, or integration. Some people joined hate groups such as the Ku Klux Klan, acting as vigilantes of racism, attacking and killing African Americans and civil rights activists. Although the violence probably haunted Kofi with flashbacks of his own country's fight for equality, he found inspiration in the dramatic struggle for change. "It was an exciting period," he recalled. "I had come from Ghana and we had just gone through our own struggle of independence. When I came to the States, the social upheaval reminded me of some of the things that had gone on in Ghana."[15] After watching his country gain independence, Kofi was probably more optimistic about the civil rights movement than his African-American friends were.

Despite his positive attitude, Kofi, too, suffered the consequences of racism. One day, Kofi was almost attacked by a white gang while walking with a white girl on the streets of Minneapolis. The incident prompted a personal apology from the mayor of the city. Overall, however, Kofi felt a sense of security and belonging on the Macalester campus. "There was a celebration of diversity throughout this student body unlike any other I have known," Kofi commented. "Students from a wide range of backgrounds and nationalities lived, worked, and grew together. We were not merely greeted with tolerance, we were welcomed with warmth."[16]

In 1961, Kofi earned his Bachelor of Arts degree in economics from Macalester College. He was ready to step out into his adult life. Although Kofi had no idea what kind of life his future held, he assumed it would be set in Ghana. He figured that after graduation he would make some money in business. Then, later in life, he would enter politics in Ghana and help develop his home country. When Kofi peered out into his distant future, he pictured himself retiring at 60, as a farmer. At 80, he'd die in bed. "But it's one of those things God does," Kofi later commented. "Our most intricate plans don't always turn out as we expected."[17] Kofi would soon find twists and turns down his road of life—and a greater significance than he could have ever imagined.

STEPPING OUT INTO THE WORLD

With diploma in hand, Kofi decided to make yet another big move. Instead of heading home, he enrolled in a graduate program at the Institut universitaire des hautes études internationales (the Graduate Institute of International Studies) in Geneva, Switzerland. Switzerland's second largest city, Geneva is nestled in the Rhône valley, between the Jura Mountains and the Alps, beside one of the largest Alpine Lakes: Lake Geneva. The school boasts a grand view of the pinnacle of Mont Blanc. Kofi was certainly impressed by the scenic parks and promenades, surrounded by breathtaking gardens. From the city streets, Kofi heard a smattering of languages—German, Italian, and French—drifting from the sidewalk cafes. Although he had to get accustomed to yet another culture, Kofi must have marveled at the grandeur of this post-graduate experience. He threw himself into his studies and completed a graduate degree in economics by 1962.

After graduation, Kofi faced a difficult decision. All through college, Kofi had planned to someday return to Ghana. Now, he had second thoughts. In Ghana, his best business prospect was a job with the Pillsbury food company. The more he thought about the position there, the more it seemed to be a dead end. In addition, during the past few years, the political situation in Ghana had become shaky.

President Kwame Nkrumah of Ghana (left), is pictured above with then UN Secretary-General Dag Hammarskjöld during his 1961 trip to New York City. After setting up a democratic government and leading Ghana through its first years of independence, President Nkrumah began building his own personal power, creating unrest within his country.

Ghanaian President Kwame Nkrumah was responsible for much of the unrest in Kofi's home country. After setting up a democratic government and leading Ghana through its early years of independence, Nkrumah began pumping up his personal power. Eventually, in 1966, a military council forced him out of office and reevaluated Ghana's constitution. Even in 1962, though, the present government was disintegrating. Kofi Annan had reservations about starting a career in his homeland, where the future seemed locked in turmoil.

Despite Nkrumah's power-hungry demise, he was responsible for the inspiration of an independent Ghana and suggesting the possibility of a united Africa. After Ghana threw off the shackles of colonial rule in 1958, Nkrumah boldly stated that Ghana's independence would prove "meaningless, unless it is linked up with the total liberation of Africa."[18] Nkrumah and his followers succeeded in bringing old colonies and new nations across the continent into an alliance. In 1963, they formed the Organization of African Unity (OAU). The OAU included 32 existing African states. Finally, after centuries of European rule, the new governments of Africa stood independent, yet united in a common goal.

Kofi Annan must have seen the importance of nations cooperating with each other, working toward peace and stability. About this time, he received a job offer so timely he could not turn it down. The United Nations wanted Annan to serve as the administrative and budget officer for the World Health Organization (WHO). This agency attacks disease problems everywhere on the globe—especially in developing countries—delivering essential drugs, providing health assistance in emergencies and natural disasters, and fighting infectious disease. WHO is the driving force behind many historic health achievements, such as the eradication of smallpox from the world in 1980. Later, WHO helped eliminate poliomyelitis from the Americas. From 1980 to 1995, UNICEF and WHO together widened immunization coverage around the world against six big killers—polio, tetanus, measles, whooping cough, diphtheria, and tuberculosis—saving the lives of 2.5 million children a year. Of course, at the time of Annan's job offer, these great feats were yet to be accomplished. The monumental goals were set, however, and Annan was up to the challenge.

Budget officer was a P1-level position—the lowest professional position within the international civil service—but the offer seemed to echo all the principles Annan held dear. Witnessing firsthand the struggle for Ghana's independence, America's civil rights movement, and the importance of international peace stressed at Macalester, the United Nations turned out to be the perfect fit for Kofi Annan. He even got a chance to help his West African home. One of the projects WHO tackled was river blindness—a crippling disease common in West Africa. No doubt Annan felt a great sense of pride knowing that, although he could do little to help Ghana's fluctuating political stability, he could at least do something to improve the living conditions of West Africans. WHO succeeded in this endeavor. Today, river blindness has been virtually eliminated from the 11 West African countries it once affected.

After three years with WHO, Annan was promoted to the Economic Commission for Africa (ECA)—stationed in Addis

The Birth of the United Nations

The idea of international peace and cooperation has been around for hundreds of years. Bringing governments from around the world together and getting them to agree on common goals, though, is no small task. At first, governments formed unions on small scales. In 1865, the International Telecommunication Union—the world's oldest intergovernmental organization—was founded in Paris. Next came the Universal Postal Union, organized in 1874. Both of these groups eventually became specialized agencies of the United Nations.

The League of Nations (forerunner of the United Nations), was established after World War I in 1919, under the Treaty of Versailles. This group attempted to settle crises peacefully, avoid war, and draw up rules for warfare, in an effort "to promote international cooperation and to achieve peace and security."* The League of Nations ceased to exist after failing to prevent World War II.

U.S. President Franklin D. Roosevelt coined the name "United Nations" in the "Declaration by United Nations" of January 1,

Ababa, Ethiopia. The ECA promotes policies that increase economic cooperation among the member countries of the United Nations, particularly focusing on production, trade, and institutional facilities. There, Annan focused his attentions on project developments for the economic and social issues of Africa. Needing more knowledge for his ever-broadening career, he traveled back to the United States, where he obtained a master's degree in management from the Massachusetts Institute of Technology.

In 1974, after nearly a decade of work in international affairs, Annan returned to Ghana, this time hoping to improve living conditions in his homeland. He became director of the Ghana Tourist Development Company. Ghana was still mired in political

---

1942. This declaration came during World War II, when representatives of 26 nations pledged that their governments would together continue to fight against the Axis Powers (Germany, Japan, and Italy).

In 1945, representatives from more than 50 countries met in San Francisco, at the United Nations Conference on International Organization, to create a charter. The delegates sifted through proposals made by the representatives of China, the Soviet Union (Russia), the United Kingdom (Britain), and the United States. All 50 representatives signed the United Nations Charter on June 26, 1945—and the United Nations was born. Poland, which was not represented at the conference, signed the charter soon afterward and also became one of the original 51 member states.

Since its creation in 1945, the United Nations has quadrupled in size, representing 99 percent of the Earth's population. Today, the United Nations boasts 191 member states.

Basic Facts About the United Nations. New York: United Nations, 2000, p. 3.

instability, though, and the government tottered between military and civilian rule, suffering one military coup after another. As tourism manager, Annan faced the difficult task of attracting foreigners to volatile Ghana. Annan later admitted, "I wanted to make a contribution to Ghana but I found myself constantly fighting the military, so I went back to the UN." In 1976, he once again returned to Geneva, with hopes of bringing peace and better living conditions to the world from within the United Nations.

CHAPTER 4

Learning the Ropes

O nce again, Annan threw himself into his work at the United Nations. For a time, he served on the Second United Nations Emergency Force (UNEF II) in Ismailia, Egypt. All the while, his experiences on the bottom rungs of the UN ladder were helping him learn the ropes for more important roles around the world. Finally, in 1980, he landed his first high-level post as the deputy director of administration and head of personnel in the Office of the UN High Commission for Refugees (UNHCR) in Geneva and the UN headquarters in New York. This department of the UN leads international action for the worldwide protection of refugees and works to solve refugee problems. Since its creation in 1950, the UNHCR has aided about 50 million refugees and has earned two Nobel Peace Prizes (in 1954 and 1981).

When Annan began working with the UNHCR, the people of Afghanistan were in crisis. Throughout the previous decade, Afghanistan had experienced political turbulence, military coups, and violence. In 1979, the Soviet Union invaded the country and took over the government. This invasion sparked the beginning of a long guerrilla war with the *mujahideen*, Muslim fighters who opposed the Communist-led government. Throughout these years of conflict and war, the people of Afghanistan faced economic hardship, fear, and an intense desire for peace. Wave upon wave of people fled their homeland, seeking refuge in surrounding countries and throughout the world. These refugees suffered hunger, droughts, and diseases. At the end of their journeys, they often did not find the peace and security they had hoped for. The UNHCR helped establish refugee camps in the neighboring country of Pakistan. As the war dragged on, many of these camps became permanent settlements for Afghanistan refugees.

At the same time, in another corner of the world, people were in the same kind of trouble. Ethiopia, in eastern Africa, is primarily a rural society. There, the lives of the peasants were rooted in the land—in farming—from which they managed to make a meager living. Throughout history, they have faced political repression, as well as countless natural disasters and military conflicts. Crops have failed because of both droughts and floods, putting the lives of hundreds of thousands in jeopardy.

In 1969, a drought hit the Sahel (the small, eastern portion of Africa that juts out into the Arabian Sea) and spread east through the horn of Africa (the zone around the southern border of the Sahara Desert). Emergency food supplies quickly ran out, and by 1973, famine threatened the lives of thousands of Ethiopian nomads, who had left their homeland and traveled to Somalia, Djibouti, Kenya, and Sudan in search of food. By the end of the year, about 300,000 peasants had died of starvation, and thousands more sought refuge in Ethiopian towns and villages.

Life looked bleak for these scavengers, but things were about to get worse. In 1974, a military regime took over Ethiopia. The new government tried to improve the lives of peasants, but famine and hunger continued to ravage the country. To make matters worse, insurgents in Eritrea, Tigray, and the Ogaden rose up against the military regime, forcing thousands of Ethiopians to flee to neighboring countries for safety. In 1977, a war broke out in the Ogaden,

Starving cattle are shown above in this 1973 photograph, wandering in the Sahel region of Senegal. In 1969, a catastrophic drought hit the Sahel and spread east through the horn of Africa, causing famine throughout the area.

followed by a drought in eastern Ethiopia. Large numbers of refugees traveled across the southeastern frontier into Somalia. When the Somali forces were defeated in the war, several hundred thousand Ethiopians again fled to Sudan. Even in the Ogaden, Somali refugee camps swelled at a rate of 1,000 newcomers a day. Many of these people suffered from dehydration, malnutrition, and diseases such as dysentery, malaria, and tuberculosis. Across the area, more than 700,000 refugees were scattered in crude camps, living in squalor with poor sanitation and diminishing food supplies, and without medical assistance. Annan's agency began a repatriation program—a plan to send refugees safely back to their homeland. This program continued well into the 1980s.

The early years of Annan's involvement with the UNHCR were successful ones. In 1978, the agency facilitated the repatriation and rehabilitation of 200,000 people from Burma who had taken refuge in Bangladesh after ethnic and religious conflicts forced them to leave their homeland. The same year, UNHCR helped 150,000 Zairian refugees living in Angola return home. Conversely, the agency helped ensure the return home of 50,000 Angolans in Zaire. In addition, 100,000 refugees from Nicaragua living in Costa Rica and Honduras were repatriated. From 1979 to 1980, refugees returned to Equatorial Guinea, Kampuchea, and Uganda. The UNHCR also extended repatriation for Ethiopian refugees and the return movement to Ethiopia began. In 1981, about 650,000 refugees and displaced people traveled back to their homes in independent Zimbabwe, a huge success for Annan and his associates—one of many that earned the UNHCR a Nobel Peace Prize in 1981.

TWO CULTURES, ONE MARRIAGE

While working for the United Nations High Commissioner for Refugees in Genevea, Annan met Nane Lagergren, a charming Swedish attorney who was also working for UNHCR. Nane is the niece of Raoul Wallenberg, a Swedish diplomat and humanitarian who mysteriously disappeared while rescuing tens of thousands of Hungarian Jews from Nazi death camps. Wallenberg had long been a role model for Annan. The couple married in 1984 at the UN chapel in New York. Annan and Nane had three children from previous marriages—Annan's daughter Ama and son Kofo from his first marriage to Titi Alakija, a Nigerian woman, and Nane's 14-year-old daughter, Nina.

After the wedding, Nane left her law practice, and the couple moved to Roosevelt Island—an interesting, historical community on an island in New York City's East River. Roosevelt Island is home to many foreign diplomats, due its proximity to the United Nations headquarters on the east side of Manhattan. There,

Annan and his wife, Nane Annan, are shown above arriving at the United Nations Mission in Angola, August 25, 2002. The couple was married in 1984, at the UN chapel in New York.

Annan worked as the director of the budget, while Nane—also a noted artist—devoted most of her time to painting. Later, when the couple lived in Sutton Place, Nane's studio had a lovely view of the UN headquarters, where the bright-colored flags of member states wave in the breeze.

In the beginning, married life was an interesting and frustrating clash of cultures. Annan described,

We would organize a dinner. Nane being a Swede—that's a country where if you invite them for 8 o'clock, they will get there five or ten to eight and circle the block, and ring the bell at eight—was used to punctuality. The Ghanaian or the African guests would come about thirty minutes to an hour late, and she used to get furious.[19]

As in most areas of Annan's life, over the years he learned the art of compromise, useful in ironing out their marital wrinkles. "I'm more punctual now," he claims. "And she's more relaxed." As a safety net, though, he offered his wife a bit of advice: "Just don't do soufflés."[20]

Today, Annan and Nane try to stay connected, despite their busy lives. They go for hikes on holidays, play tennis, and take walks through Central Park; snapping pictures along the way is a favorite pastime. For relaxation, they read together. Most of all, Annan comments, "We laugh a lot, at ourselves and at situations."[21]

PERSIAN GULF WAR: UN MEANS BUSINESS

From 1987 to 1990, Annan served as the assistant secretary-general for human resources management and as the security coordinator for the UN system. During his service, Annan faced his greatest challenge yet, one that would place him in the international spotlight.

From 1980 to 1988, Iran and Iraq had been engaged in a bloody war that cost the lives of more than a million people. In 1988, the United Nations drew up a cease-fire agreement that was accepted by both sides, but it was of little comfort. The war had resolved nothing between the two nations. The agreement merely brought an end to the fighting, and instead, left countries in the Persian Gulf region competing with each other in an arms race. A stalemate between the two nations was left like a rumbling volcano on the cusp of a fiery eruption.

In 1990, Iraqi leader Saddam Hussein was eager to flex his muscles again. Hussein had risen to power as leader of the Ba'ath

Socialist Party and the military dictator of Iraq, in a postcolonial atmosphere of paranoia and political threats. Iraq is located in what was the Fertile Crescent of ancient Babylonian emperors and was once a wealthy country. During the first half of the twentieth century, French and British colonialists tore the country apart, creating boundaries that served their own interests rather than the ethnic and economic needs of the region. Over time, ethnic and religious divisions swelled into chasms of disarray and instability. Iraqis saw its petite neighbor, Kuwait, as a man-made state carved out of Iraq's natural coastline—perhaps its sole purpose being to prevent the Persian Gulf's oil fields from falling under the control of a single country. Aside from coveting Kuwait's wealth, Hussein hated its government, a monarchy, even though he had accepted billions of dollars in aid from it to support his army during the war with Iran. In 1990, Hussein was ready to build a war machine that would make him the most feared mastermind throughout the region. Creating this kind of force not only required a power-ful army and arsenals of weapons, but also money and oil. So, he looked to a country that had both—Kuwait.

Over the years, Iraq repeatedly harassed Kuwait, mostly over border disputes. Iraq insisted that the Bubiyan and Warbah Islands at the mouth of the Shatt al-Arab waterway were within Iraqi borders. Controlling these islands would secure for Iraq a highly desirable passageway to the Persian Gulf. Hussein falsely accused Kuwait of stealing oil from Iraq and threatened military action. In August 1988, Kuwait claimed that Iraqi troops backed by gunboats had attacked Bubiyan; they called on the United Nations for help. UN investigators tracked the so-called Iraqi troops to fishing boats and figured they were simply scavenging for weapons and supplies. The United Nations accused Kuwait of "crying wolf" in a desperate ploy to secure international support. Therefore, the Iraqi invasion of Kuwait on August 2, 1990, stunned the world.

The Iraqi Republican Guard made a swift drive toward Saudi oil fields and shipping terminals. Apparently, Hussein was mak-ing a move to control the world's oil supply, but perhaps his vision was wider—perhaps he meant to unify the Arabs against the West in the process. He made a gross miscalculation, however.

Hussein assumed his fellow Arabs would simply tolerate his seizure of Kuwait rather than call on the outside world for help. He was wrong. Instead, with the government of Kuwait in exile, frightened King Fahd of Saudi Arabia (whose country borders Iraq to the south) looked at once to the United States and the United Nations for support. U.S. President George H.W. Bush, together with the British and Soviet governments, condemned Hussein's actions, and Annan's UN Security Council demanded Iraqi troops immediately withdraw from Kuwait. Hussein did not flinch.

On the same day, King Fahd requested American military protection, and President Bush took action. Operation Desert Shield deployed 200,000 American troops—supplemented by British, French, and Saudi allied units—to the northern deserts of Saudi Arabia. This deployment was the largest American overseas operation since the Vietnam War, but Hussein was unimpressed with this response. On August 8, he annexed Kuwait and declared it Iraq's nineteenth province. The UN Security Council was appalled, and member nations began offering their help and support to the cause. When Hussein's standoff met with continued resistance, he took the showdown one step further. He detained as hostages all foreigners stuck in Kuwait and Iraq and rescinded permanent peace with Iran, freeing his army of half a million for battle.

The United Nations voted to enforce an international embargo, banning member nations from exporting goods to Iraq and forbidding them from purchasing Iraqi oil. By withholding everyday supplies and refusing to buy oil, essentially hurting the Iraqi economy, the United Nations hoped Hussein would reconsider and pull his troops out of Kuwait. Still, Hussein ignored the demands and refused to retreat, proclaiming, "The great, the jewel, and the mother of battles has begun."[22]

In the wake of the cold war, it seemed as though this conflict was a test of the United Nations. Would it prove to be a genuine force for peace and justice? Surprisingly, the United Nations had full Soviet and Western cooperation in this matter. In fact, a UN coalition against Iraq seemed to be the most important key to victory. On August 25, the Security Council agreed to allow Allied ships in the Persian Gulf to enforce the embargo against Iraq, using force if necessary.

In early September, Hussein began releasing foreigners being held in Kuwait—quelling some fears that there would be a prolonged hostage crisis. This first act of leniency raised UN hopes that Hussein might be open to diplomatic negotiations and ultimately stand down. He did not release all hostages detained behind Iraqi lines, however, and still made no moves to withdraw from Kuwait. The United Nations could not easily forget about the thousands of foreigners, including hundreds of UN workers, who were stilled trapped in Kuwait and Iraq. Someone needed to get those hostages released. UN Secretary-General Javier Pérez de Cuéllar appointed Annan to head negotiations with Hussein for release of the hostages. As Annan prepared for his crucial talk, war continued to loom in the Persian Gulf. On November 29, the Security Council gave the United States authorization to use all means necessary if Iraq failed to comply with UN resolutions by January 15, 1991.

On the evening of January 16, Annan sat on a plane headed for Baghdad. Hussein was still on the warpath, with no apparent intention to stand down. On the eve of his first major diplomatic mission, Annan appeared calm and controlled. Deep down, his stomach must have twisted as he contemplated the lives at stake. One of his aides broke Annan's thoughtful stare. "What if it doesn't work?" she asked. "What kind of contingency planning can we do?" Almost as if he was shocked she could ask such a thing, Annan fired back, "Don't ever speak to me negatively when I'm about to negotiate. We'll make it—and I don't want to hear that we may not make it."[23] Annan did make it, eventually. In the end, all hostages were released, including the 900 UN workers. The negotiations were an extraordinary victory for the United Nations. In fact, Annan's success earned him a new position—

The Cold War Brings Drama to the United Nations

After World War II, a cold war—as opposed to a hot, active war, such as the world wars—developed between the United States and the Soviet Union, plus their respective allies. The struggle was called the cold war because it never actually led to a direct armed conflict between the superpowers on a wide scale. Rather, it was waged by means of economic pressure, diplomatic maneuvering, propaganda, assassination, and low-intensity military operations from 1947 until the collapse of the Soviet Union in 1991. Although the cold war never resulted in a full-scale world war, the Korean War, the Hungarian Revolution, the Cuban Missile Crisis, the Vietnam War, the Afghan War, and civil wars in countries such as Angola, El Salvador, and Nicaragua were some occasions when cold war tensions turned into armed conflict.

When the major European empires began to disintegrate after World War II, a series of power vacuums developed, which needed to be filled in some way. The United Nations looked for a new approach to its organization, because the original structure of the UN Charter was ineffective. When the UN was created, President Roosevelt called on "the four policemen," the alliance that had won the war—the United States, the Soviet Union, Britain, and China—to remain unified to supervise and, if necessary, enforce the peace of the world. During the cold war, however, these former allies were enemies, engaged in a buildup of nuclear arms and rocketry (which led to the Space Race), missiles, submarines, jet fighters, bombers, and chemical and biological weapons, yet none wanted to be dragged into a nuclear conflict. The two superpowers that emerged—the United States and the Soviet Union—brought their frosty tensions and paranoia to the United Nations.

Soviet Premier Nikita Khrushchev became famous for angry outbursts and repeated disruptions during meetings of the General Assembly. When he disagreed with the way the United Nations was handling conflicts and crises, he would begin shouting in Russian and pound his fists on the table. Probably the most

Soviet Premier Nikita Khruschev, pictured above, pounds his desk at the UN General Assembly to indicate his disapproval of a speech by UN Secretary-General Dag Hammarskjöld, October 3, 1960. Khruschev's disruptive behavior at the United Nations would gain notoriety during the cold war.

memorable incident in UN cold war history was when a Filipino delegate accused the USSR of imperialism in Eastern Europe. Khrushchev slammed his fist on the desk and shouted insults at the delegate—calling him "a jerk, a stooge, and a lackey of imperialism." He then removed one of his shoes and banged it on the table. On another occasion, he said, "We will bury you"; this was directed at the United States and capitalism. He also became famous for boasting to the U.S. president, "Our rockets could hit a fly over the United States."* With so much drama in the United Nations, the end of the cold war must have brought members a sigh of relief.

*"Nikita Khrushchev," Wikipedia. Available at http://en.wikipedia.org/wiki/Nikita_Khrushchev.

assistant secretary-general for program planning, budget and finance. His diplomatic efforts proved he was much too talented to stay stuck in budgets and numbers for long, however.

Unfortunately, Annan's talks did not bring peace in the gulf. On the night of January 17, coalition forces struck Baghdad with the first air attack of Operation Desert Storm. A month later, on February 24, coalition troops started a massive ground assault, smashing the links between Iraqi forces in Kuwait and their bases in Iraq. Just two days later, Hussein announced that Iraqi troops were leaving Kuwait. Although he still refused to admit personal failure, Hussein abruptly agreed to abide by the UN resolutions on March 3. On April 11, Annan and the Security Council declared that Desert Storm was over.

The Persian Gulf War proved to be an American and United Nations victory. The Iraqis suffered more than 100,000 casualties, to the Allies' count of about 340 killed. The war turned out to be the most one-sided major engagement in the history of modern warfare. Kuwait was free, despite major damage in part due to the Iraqi "scorched-earth" policy, which included torching hundreds of oil wells. Above all, the United Nations presented itself as genuinely united and true to its word—backing up its resolutions with force. The war did not accomplish one great goal, however. Hussein was still in power and hungry for payback.

CHAPTER 5

The Trouble With Peacekeeping

Javier Pérez de Cuéllar's term as secretary-general expired in 1991, and the UN General Assembly elected former university professor and Egyptian minister of state Boutros Boutros-Ghali to take his place. As secretary-general, Boutros-Ghali was active and aggressive as well as introverted and moody, and he sometimes acted aloof. His intellectual arrogance was often abrasive. When logic took over, he was convinced that his analysis was right. Boutros-Ghali's presence startled critics, and many people inflated his influence. UN officials accused him of trying to become "chief executive of the world" and "the world's commander-in-chief."[24] The secretary-general ran the UN on instincts and suspicion. At times, Boutros-Ghali could be charming and witty, and his mind analyzed information with sharp brilliance. He could absorb data and sort it into policy with ease.

Above all, Boutros-Ghali was fiercely self-reliant. "There's a joke," said an ambassador on the Security Council, "that whenever the Secretary-General wants to look for someone he can trust, he stands up on his two feet, walks across the room to the wall,

United Nations Secretary-General Boutros Boutros-Ghali sits at his desk at the UN in December 1996. Boutros-Ghali, a former university professor and Egyptian minister of state, was chosen for the position of secretary-general in 1991.

and looks into the mirror."[25] He became the most stubbornly independent secretary-general in the 50-year history of the United Nations.

At the time when Boutros-Ghali stepped into office, a new type of crisis began to appear within international politics. Instead of major wars between powerful nations, regional conflicts between ethnic and religious groups erupted all over the world. These sects did not follow international laws and had little respect for the United Nations. Feuding cultures would put the United Nations to the test.

The United Nations' most valuable and important role is peacekeeping. In its first 40 years, the Security Council authorized only 13 peacekeeping operations. During the organization's fifth decade, an additional 20 plans were launched, half under Boutros-Ghali. In June 1992—after six months on the job—Boutros-Ghali presented his "Agenda for Peace." His proposal was in response to the Security Council's desire to expand "the capacity of the United Nations for preventive diplomacy, for peacemaking and for peacekeeping."[26]

Although "Agenda for Peace" was a grand title, his proposal was less than radical, mainly reiterating what UN peacekeepers had been doing all along: the traditional monitoring of cease-fire lines. The plan, however, did break new ground in three areas: (1) preventive deployment of troops to an area of potential crisis when a worried government asks for them to discourage an outbreak of hostilities, (2) agreements with governments to set aside special troops for possible rapid deployment by the UN in peacekeeping and other military missions, and (3) use of peace-enforcement troops, more heavily armed than peacemakers, for dangerous military missions like the forcible maintenance of a cease-fire.[27]

Boutros-Ghali would not have to wait long to see whether or not his policies would be success. Three post–cold war peacekeeping missions were just around the corner, ready to challenge Annan and the United Nations.

SOMALIA NIGHTMARE

On January 3, 1993, people of Somalia surrounded the UN compound in the capital city of Mogadishu. They hurled garbage and rocks at the building, shouting curses and "Boutros-Ghali down!"[28] The angry mob believed the secretary-general favored the enemies of their leader, General Muhammad Farrah Aideed. The riot forced Boutros-Ghali to abandon his plans to stop at the compound for a meeting with UN staff members there. Two days later, he spoke to Somalian warlords at a peace conference in Addis Ababa, Ethiopia. The meeting opened in confusion and discord and the group made little headway. As Boutros-Ghali was preparing to leave Addis Ababa, he used a final news conference to condemn the Somalis' actions. He begged them to understand that outsiders in Somalia—U.S. Marines, the UN and humanitarian relief organizations—offered the people one last chance for peace. If Somalia could establish a workable, peaceful government, the outsiders would pack up and leave. "The Cold War is finished," Boutros-Ghali explained. "Nobody wants control over Somalia. . . . No one is interested in Somalia, not for strategic reasons, not for oil, not for gold. . . . There can be a real *drame* [the French world for "tragedy"] someday: The world could forget Somalia in a few minutes."[29]

At that time, however, there was no logic in Somalia. For years, many Africans had believed Somalia was blessed, because it had escaped the curse of tribalism. Unlike most African countries, Somalia had only one tribe, one religion, and one language. Still oddly, clans and subclans were at war with each other. Not one sliver of difference separated them ideologically. They only scrambled for power—no clan wanted another to have the upper hand.

The roots of the Somalia crisis were buried deep in the repressive 21-year rule of General Muhammad Siad Barre, who seized power in a coup in 1969. Somalia had been known since its independence in 1960 as an impoverished but rowdy nation in the horn of Africa. Somalian warlords made noisy boasts of plans to swallow up petite Djibouti, the northern portion of Kenya, and the Ogaden region of Ethiopia. For decades, Somalia fought

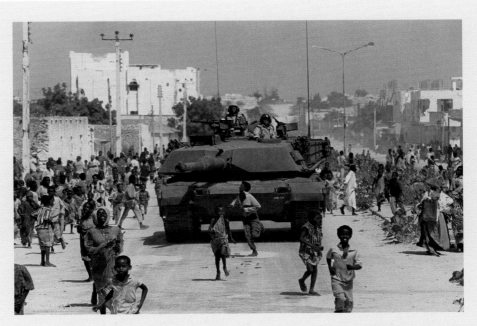

Somali children run alongside a U.S. Marine tank during an armored patrol in north Mogadishu, Somalia, in January 1993. The United States first sent troops into Somalia in 1992, as part of a relief mission.

a bloody war with Ethiopia. In the beginning, the United States backed Ethiopia, whereas the Soviet Union supported Somalia. When the Ethiopian emperor was overthrown, the new government despised his ties with the United States, and the Soviets switched their support to Ethiopia. At this point, the United States felt it had no other choice but to back Somalia, or the two countries would surely fall into conflict with each other. The United States began pumping military equipment and money into Somalia. When civil war exploded in the late 1980s, the country was stocked with weaponry.

Muhammad Siad Barre was a southerner who favored his own clan. It did not take long for resentment to grow barbs in the north. When rebellion erupted, Barre responded by shelling northern cities. At the end of it all, the main city of Hargeisa had been reduced to rubble, and thousands of civilians lay dead in the streets. Three hundred thousand refugees fled to Ethiopia for safety. Paranoid about further uprisings, Barre began to depend even more on his own clan, alienating other clans and subclans in the south. Finally, they, too, revolted against him. In early 1991, Barre and his army fled Mogadishu and made a break for Bardera. Taking place during the height of the Persian Gulf War, the news went virtually unnoticed.

Barre tried to reorganize and retake Mogadishu, but Aideed— a former general in Barre's army—and his rebel militia drove him back, this time for good. With Barre finally ousted, seeking refuge in Nigeria, the warlords who overthrew him turned against each other. Aideed led the strongest faction, but it was not powerful enough to control the entire country. Aideed saw himself as the savior of Somalia, however, and the true ruler of the land. Aideed's prime rival was Ali Mahdi Muhammad, a Mogadishu businessman whose forces controlled the northern quarters of the capital. In May 1991, at a conference in Djibouti, Ali Mahdi proclaimed himself president of Somalia. Aideed, believing the meeting was fixed, boycotted the conference.

The civil war took a devastating toll on Somalia. A UN report called the country "a human disaster of appalling magnitude" and "a nightmare of bloodshed and brutality."[30] While the rest of the world took little notice, Boutros-Ghali tried to keep a close eye on the situation. He even scolded the ambassadors of the Security Council for paying attention to troubles in Bosnia while ignoring war-torn Somalia. In March, he sent Muhammad Sahnoun, an experienced Algerian diplomat, to Somalia as his special representative. Under further pressure from the secretary-general, the Security Council authorized a UN peacekeeping mission to Somalia in late April 1992. In order to carry out the mission, though, the UN would have to gain approval from the warlords. The first contingent of 500 armed Pakistani soldiers did not arrive in Somalia until September. By this time, the first American official to report on the crisis in Somalia described it as "the world's worst humanitarian disaster." He warned that three out of every four children under the age of five might die in as little as six months if they did not receive food and medical attention.[31]

The United States immediately began airlifting food into Mombasa, on the coast of Kenya. For six months, American planes flew tens of thousands of metric tons of food from Mombasa to Somalia. But looting and hijacking ran rampant. Gunmen demanded landing fees from the pilots, forcing relief workers to arm their jeeps and Land Rovers with heavy weapons and military escorts.

Meanwhile, Sahnoun worked feverishly with Aideed and other warlords to get them to call off their dragoons and allow peacekeepers into Somalia. The UN representative became increasingly frustrated with the dragging feet of UN bureaucrats, however, who shipped out meager supplies to a ravaged country. He vented his exasperation on American television, admonishing the United Nations for its failures. The incident infuriated Boutros-Ghali, who responded to Sahnoun with a stern scolding. In response, Sahnoun shot back a letter of resignation. UN diplomats tried to persuade them to work out their differences, but the two stubborn men would not budge. Sahnoun left Somalia and the United Nations with a hole in the center of an already crumbling situation. The UN felt pressure building with more intensity each day, as camera crews filled televisions around the world with images of starving children—potbellied from malnutrition, sunken-faced, and bony. People watched with growing anger, wondering why nothing was being done. Back at the United Nations, Boutros-Ghali was searching for a new right-hand man to handle this escalating tragedy. On March 1, 1993, he promoted Kofi Annan to the hot seat—assistant secretary-general for peacekeeping. All eyes looked to Annan to restore peace.

HUNT FOR AIDEED

Following the Persian Gulf War, the United States pulled back from the United Nations. After using the UN for support in the war, the action almost came as a slap in the face. To many UN workers, it seemed as though the United States only found the UN useful if it could serve America's purposes. The wealthiest and most powerful nation in the world was refusing to invest as much money or as many workers in the organization as it had in the past.

Still, the United States did not turn its back on the rest of the world. As the media exposed the widening gap of the Somalia crisis, the U.S. Congress and American relief organizations realized they must do something to save Somalia. President Bush informed Boutros-Ghali that the United States was prepared to deploy up to 30,000 troops to Somalia. Although some UN officials believed the United Nations could handle the disaster alone, Boutros-Ghali disagreed. In his mind, a U.S. intervention was the only solution. At the same time, he did not want a replay of the Persian Gulf War—America obtaining the go-ahead from the United Nations, only to walk away at the end of it all. The secretary-general devised an elaborate set of restrictions, reporting requirements, and strategies for the American-led mission.

The first wave of U.S. soldiers was dispatched in December 1992. Americans envisioned their troops swooping in with bundles of food to make a quick rescue of those frail children, then returning home. The secretary-general's requirements were not that simple, however. In a letter to the Security Council, Boutros-Ghali insisted that it was necessary to bring peace to Somalia on a lasting basis and end the violence against international relief efforts. In order to achieve this, the heavy weapons of the factions must be neutralized and brought under international control. Also, the gangs and irregular forces would need to be disarmed. The resolution passed by the Security Council was far less explicit about the disarmament requirements, however. Boutros-Ghali understood that the UN could not take over after the American-led forces if a peaceful environment was not secured. The Bush administration—not wanting to get tied into a long-term conflict that could include U.S. casualties—disagreed.

Boutros-Ghali wrote a letter to President Bush explaining the resolution in UN terms: It was not enough for the Americans to provide security just for the delivery of food. The letter infuriated the Bush administration, which accused the secretary-general of trying to change the goalposts in the middle of the game. In truth, Boutros-Ghali's interpretation of the resolution was probably closer to its intent than the American view. In any case, the UN's hands were tied. After all, they could not force the United States to do anything it did not want to do.

President Bush's special envoy rushed to Mogadishu to convince Aideed and Ali Mahdi to hold their fire while American troops and allies came ashore in Somalia. The two warlords were easily persuaded—they certainly did not want to ruffle American feathers. The United States had no intention of engaging in a mass disarmament: As long as the Somalis kept their weapons out of sight, they were not taken away. On occasion, the Americans did seize heavy weapons that were either out in the open or causing trouble. As a matter of principle, the U.S. envoy tried to persuade the warlords to turn over their weaponry. Ali Mahdi gave his up to the intervention force for storage, but Aideed claimed his stock had disappeared. The envoy did not press the issue with Aideed, since in American terms, it was technically none of his business.

Within a few months, the atmosphere of Somalia had undergone a miraculous overhaul. Violence vanished with the soldiers present, and food stocks swiftly made it to the needy. With everything seemingly in place, Washington called for the United Nations to take over the operation. The Americans managed to persuade Boutros-Ghali to replace Marrack Goulding, then the under-secretary-general for peacekeeping, with Annan. They thought soft-spoken Annan would be more amenable to American suggestions for the peacekeepers. Like the Americans, Annan also believed the UN should hold the authority to enforce the peace in Somalia.

Still, Boutros-Ghali felt uneasy about the takeover. He felt the United States had failed to establish a secure environment, as they were obligated to do. The conditions, according to Boutros-Ghali, were still volatile, and disarmament was far from complete. Nevertheless, the Security Council authorized a UN takeover in May 1993.

The official transfer took place on May 4, with a force of 28,000, plus the American Quick Reaction Force, equipped with helicopters, tanks, trucks, and Bradley assault vehicles. The Security Council, now under Annan's direction, gave peace-keepers the authority to do battle on the warlords, if needed, to end any chaos in Somalia. Aideed soon realized that the UN's policies and plans for disarmament would weaken his political standing in Somalia. He immediately began a series of games to undermine the UN mission.

Radio Mogadishu, controlled by Aideed, launched a hate campaign, labeling representatives of the United Nations and United States as aggressors and colonial imperialists. He pleaded with Somalis to remember the glorious days of their past, when they fought against foreign domination. Not needing such publicity, UN forces made plans to knock out the radio station under the guise of a routine weapons inspection. When Somalis got wind of the ruse, hostile crowds gathered in the streets, setting up roadblocks to prevent inspection teams from returning to their barracks. Aideed's militiamen crept onto the scene, ducking behind women and children while they waited for an opportunity to attack. Suddenly, the militia opened fire on UN peace enforcers. At the end of the day, 24 Pakistani peace enforcers were dead, 57 more injured, and 6 taken hostage. Shocked at the apparent arsenal Aideed had tucked away, the United Nations vowed justice for the "gallant soldiers [who] were murdered as they sought to serve the neediest people in the city."[32] The skirmish ignited a UN hunt for Aideed.

For the next four months, the UN fought a war with the elusive Aideed and his army. At the UN's request, the U.S. military sent 400 Rangers and Delta Force antiterrorist commandos. The hunt opened into a street war. There were hundreds of Somali casualties, as well as UN, American, Nigerian, and Pakistani deaths. As the bodies mounted, Congress became increasingly puzzled. They just could not fathom how there could be so much killing during a peacekeeping mission. The new Clinton administration had doubts about this futile manhunt. In order to put an end to the madness, they proposed a cease-fire in the Mogadishu street war and open-door talks with Aideed's faction. Secretary-General Boutros-Ghali, however, would accept nothing less than Aideed's exile.

Boutros-Ghali had a couple reasons for staying on the hunt. For starters, if the UN backed down, he might lose members' support for the Somalia mission, ultimately forcing the Security Council to withdraw completely from Somalia. This consequence would have a two-fold effect. "Not only would that condemn the people of Somalia to a resumption of civil war and all the horrors that would result," he said. "It would also represent a humbling of the United Nations." He insisted that it would have a "devastating effect" on the UN's ability to create a better world.[33]

The dragging search for Aideed had Annan's energy tapped as well. His powerlessness seemed to squeeze all hope from him. "One time, during the beginning of the Somalia crisis," he recalled sadly,

> I went to walk in the woods with my phone. It rang, and I picked up, giving some instructions. Then I walked some more. After a while, I could hear the phone trying to ring. I looked down at the phone, and it said 'low battery.' I thought [pointing to his heart], this battery is low too.[34]

Any hope that still flickered would soon be snuffed out.

UN FAILURE

At this point, the United States was feeling a bit shocked and betrayed. They did not anticipate U.S. casualties. The fact remained that the United States could have called off the hunt for Aideed at any time and pulled troops out of Somalia. The commandos and Rangers on the hunt were under the command of Major General William F. Garrison, who reported directly to the U.S. Central Command in Tampa, Florida. Therefore, they were

Influences on the Peacemaker

Secretary-General Dag Hammarskjöld poses outside the UN headquarters buildings in New York City in this 1956 photograph. During Hammarskjöld's term as secretary-general, Annan was in college. Annan would be influenced greatly by Hammarskjöld's ideals and visions for the United Nations.

When Kofi Annan was attending college, Dag Hammarskjöld was the UN secretary-general. Hammarskjöld was a man whose ideals and visions greatly influenced Annan and determined the kind of secretary-general he would later become. Hammarskjöld, the son of Hjalmar Hammarskjöld, prime minister of Sweden, was born on July 29, 1905. After representing Sweden as a delegate to the United Nations, he was elected secretary-general in 1953.

Before Hammarskjöld, the activities of the UN mostly centered around ambassadors attending conferences. When Hammarskjöld stepped into his post at age 43, the UN was mired in low morale and heavy defeatism. Hammarskjöld was an intellectual in action. He had lofty goals for the United Nations and a great passion for the organization, which quickly won the admiration of many. He had an incredible intelligence for thinking things through: for figuring out the best action to take, how to get there, and what not officially part of the UN mission. No one in Washington ordered Garrison to abort his mission, however. On the afternoon of October 3, 1993, Washington was wishing it had.

In the Sunday afternoon heat, a fleet of helicopters lowered onto a building in south Mogadishu. Delta commandos and

challenges might be faced along the way. With an unmatched zeal for the UN, he held the Charter as sacred text, something to be respected and protected at all costs. Like Annan, he was a quiet man, but extremely strong minded.

Throughout his term as secretary-general, Hammarskjöld kept believing in what the UN could be—a key to solving problems. He set in motion a plan to achieve a long-term goal: to take the institutional setup of the General Assembly, Security Council, Secretariat, and all the other organs of the UN, and shape it into a constitutional, legal mechanism. Ultimately, he had visions of installing an international law that was enforceable. Yet Hammarskjöld was far from starry-eyed. He was pragmatic and sometimes hard headed.

During his tenure as secretary-general, Hammarskjöld helped negotiate the release of American soldiers captured by the Chinese in the Korean War. He sometimes got into trouble in peacekeeping and handling crises—he had a method of trying different approaches, which frustrated some, but he insisted it was part of the UN's growing process. Hammarskjöld was also a champion of preventative diplomacy, a torch that Annan would pick up years later. In July 1960, he headed an attempt to end the Congo Civil War. He arranged for a peacekeeping force to be sent to the region. Before the troops could be deployed, however, fighting broke out between Katangese troops and the noncombatant UN forces. In an effort to secure a cease-fire, Hammarskjöld scheduled a meeting with Congo President Moise Tshombe. While en route to his peacekeeping mission on September 17, 1961, Hammarskjöld was killed when his plane crashed near Ndola Airport. He was the only secretary-general other than Annan to receive the Nobel Peace Prize, which he was awarded after his death.

Rangers jumped out and rushed inside to arrest 24 of Aideed's associates. Two of the lieutenants were so high ranking that at first the American raid appeared to be an amazing success. Perhaps their capture would smoke Aideed out of his hiding place.

Suddenly, heavily armed rebels surrounded the area, shooting down one helicopter with a rocket-propelled grenade. About 90 Rangers and commandos made their way to the fallen helicopter in hopes of saving any survivors. They formed a perimeter around the crash to protect the crew while they awaited reinforcements. A convoy of trucks was ordered to the crash site, but the trucks were abruptly halted by Somali gunmen. Another helicopter then crashed about a half-mile away. When soldiers tried to reach the wreckage, they were gunned down. The Quick Reaction Force tried to push through Somali ambushes to rescue the Rangers and commandos, but failed. Finally, at 7:00 A.M.—15 hours after the raid started—the survivors were rescued with tanks. Eighteen Americans died in the entanglement, and 84 more were wounded. To amplify the event, American television aired a scene of Somalis dragging a dead American body through the streets.

President Bill Clinton immediately called all American troops to withdraw from Somalia. The decision shocked Boutros-Ghali. No doubt Annan knew this was the prelude to a disaster. Without the Americans, the mission would be crippled and viewed around the world as a failure. To make matters worse, the United States passed stringent new guidelines for American support and participation in UN peacekeeping operations. The UN feared it would be difficult to convince other governments to support the Somali effort if the United States pulled out. Annan commented, "Other presidents and prime ministers are going to have difficulty explaining to their people that the American president is removing his troops because it is too dangerous but is encouraging them to send their own troops."[35]

Thus began the United Nations' own long and humiliating retreat. In late November 1994, the Security Council suspended all charges against Aideed and his army, ending the hunt. Aideed returned to public life, slinging threats and plotting his rise to power. More than 140 peacekeepers died during the operations. Despite the apparent failure, the UN claimed the intervention saved "hundreds of thousands of lives . . . from starvation" and had "offered a helping hand and, in the face of violent opposition firmly held that hand open for over two years, ready and willing to help." The warlords were still not settled, and the horror of civil war could swoop in for an encore at any moment. For the rest of the world, the secretary-general's words seemed all too prophetic—Somalia would be forgotten in a few minutes. The sting of failure would be felt by both the United Nations and United States for years to come. The lack of success in Somalia and later Rwanda almost led to Annan's downfall. The trouble with peacekeeping is sometimes it just cannot be kept. Sometimes, people do not want peace, especially if it is coupled with fear. Now dangling from the ropes, Annan needed a lifeline.

RWANDA MASSACRE

Ethnic tension is nothing new in Rwanda. Ongoing disagreements have caused the Hutus and Tutsis, two of the major ethnic groups in Rwanda, to knock heads for years. After the colonial period, however, the hate intensified. Although the Hutus and Tutsis share the same language, inhabit the same area, and follow the same traditions, the Belgians saw two ethnic groups when they arrived in 1916. To segregate the two, the Belgians distributed identity cards that classified each person according to his or her ethnicity. The Belgians considered the Tutsis as superior to the Hutus. For 20 years, colonialists favored Tutsis for jobs and education, whereas they discriminated against the Hutus.

Naturally, resentment mounted with the Hutus, finally erupting in a series of deadly riots in 1959. More than 20,000 Tutsis were killed, and many more fled to the neighboring countries of Burundi, Tanzania, and Uganda. When Rwanda gained independence in 1962, the Hutus took power and, for the decades that followed, used the Tutsis as scapegoats for every crisis.

As Rwanda's economic situation worsened, Hutu President Juvénal Habyarimana began to lose popularity. Meanwhile, Tutsi refugees in Uganda—supported by some moderate Hutus—formed the Rwanda Patriotic Front (RPF). They sought to overthrow Habyarimana and secure their right to return home. When Habyarimana discovered the plot, he used the intelligence as a way to win back dissident Hutus, and he accused Tutsis living in Rwanda of being RPF conspirators.

After several attacks and months of negotiations, Habyarimana and leaders of the RPF signed a peace accord in August 1993. This treaty did little to stop unrest in the country, however. A small, ineffectual UN peacekeeping group arrived on the scene to maintain a fragile truce between the two tribes. Annan, who was the head of peacekeeping at the time, was frustrated that the Security Council had not been willing to send an adequately equipped and forceful mission. Instead, he was forced to do peacekeeping "on the cheap." Then, in early April 1994, Habyarimana's plane, also carrying many of his chief staff members, was shot down. Those responsible for the shooting have never been found, but whomever it was, the killing triggered catastrophic consequences.

Back at the United Nations, Annan received a desperate plea for help. The general in charge of the UN mission received information from an informant in Rwanda that a massacre was imminent. He quickly faxed the information to Annan. Immediately, Annan sent a request to New York for permission to try to seize the weapons of the killers, but the request was denied. For the UN peacekeeping department, this was a huge mistake.

In Kigali, the Rwandan capital, the presidential guard immediately went on the warpath, first murdering leaders of the opposition, then turning on Tutsis and moderate Hutus. Within hours, they had dispatched recruits all over Rwanda to carry out a wave of slaughter. Early organizers consisted of military officers, politicians, and businessmen, but many others soon joined forces with the mayhem. Encouraged by the presidential guard and radio propaganda, an unofficial militia group called the *Interahamwe* (meaning "those who attack together") mobilized. At its peak, the Interahamwe reached 30,000 strong. Adding to the chaos, soldiers and police officers pressured ordinary citizens to join. In some cases, the Interahamwe forced civilians to murder their Tutsi neighbors.

On April 6, Hutu extremists began a genocide of the Tutsi tribe. Absolutely horrified when the killing began, Annan phoned about 100 countries, trying to get them to send more peacekeeping troops. Instead, most countries tried to get their soldiers out of the country. The United States, still feeling the sting of the Somalia expedition, shied away from Rwanda. After 10 Belgian peacekeepers were killed, the UN, without support and no other choice, withdrew most of its forces. The carnage that followed was unimaginable. During a 100-day span between April and June, some 800,000 Tutsi were brutally murdered, most of them hacked to death. Thousands of bodies littered the countryside.

Finally, in July 1994, the RPF captured Kigali, and the Hutu government collapsed, bringing an end to a deadly campaign. As soon as the RPF emerged as the clear victors, 2 million Hutus fled to Zaire (present-day Democratic Republic of Congo). Many of these refugees included insurgents involved in the massacre.

UN troops made their way back to Rwanda, a little too late, to help maintain order and restore basic services. As soon as news of the genocide spread, Annan faced a firing squad of criticism. The world had stood by, the United States and Europe not wanting to get involved, and now Annan's department had so much to answer for. Instead of hiding behind excuses, he accepted the criticism and responsibility for the atrocity. "It was a nightmare," Annan remembered. "If we had acted earlier, we could have saved a lot of lives."[36] He continued, "If ever, and God forbid, we are confronted with this sort of situation again, we do not fail—we do not fail to save lives, we do not fail to act."[37]

The trouble with the United Nations is that it has no standing army to send in at a moment's notice. The organization depends on its member states to come to the rescue. The under secretary-general of political affairs compared the role of the United Nations to a game of rugby. In rugby, if a player throws a ball to somebody who is about to be hit hard by a bunch of defenders, it's called a "hospital pass." He said the UN often gets the hospital pass. Annan believes that if the UN Security Council can be consistent in action, states bent on criminal behavior will be forced to stop. At the same time, if a Rwanda would happen again tomorrow, he sadly wonders if the international community would be there.

The massacre in Rwanda was the greatest catastrophe in UN history. Since the genocide, 500 criminals have been sentenced to death, and 100,000 are still in prison. Some of the ringleaders managed to escape, though, and many Rwandans who lost loved ones still wait for justice.

CHAPTER 6

Bosnia:
Hot Potato

While the street war raged in Somalia, the fires of another brutal catastrophe blazed in Western Europe. No one seemed to want to aggressively deal with the conflict. The risk was too bloody. Instead, Europe and the United States tossed the Bosnia crisis around like a hot potato. Once again, the UN stepped in to do whatever it could to save Bosnia—but without a "world" of support. Because Annan did not have European and U.S. backing, the Bosnian crisis turned out to be one of his most frustrating missions.

Bosnia was once part of the former Yugoslavia. The Socialist Federal Republic of Yugoslavia was a post–World War II Communist federation that included the six countries of Slovenia, Croatia, Macedonia, Montenegro, Serbia, and Bosnia and Herzegovina (commonly shortened to just "Bosnia"). In the early 1990s, the Yugoslav federation was pulled apart by a series of successions that resulted in a brutal tug-of-war for dominance.

The Bosnia crisis grew from the rule of Slobodan Milosevic, an authoritarian banker who came to power in 1987, first as leader of the Serbian League of Communists and then as president of Serbia.

Former Yugoslav President Slobodan Milosevic is pictured above, during the 2001 UN war crimes tribunal in the Hague. Milosevic died of a heart attack in prison before the end of his trial in front of the tribunal. He was accused of 66 counts of genocide, war crimes, and crimes against humanity.

Milosevic was a powerful speaker who stoked the coals of Serbian nationalism, igniting in the Serbs a fiery loyalty and pride. Croatia responded to Milosevic's rise to power by electing its own extreme nationalist in 1990—Franjo Tudjman, a former Communist and general. Tudjman held a great deal of contempt for the Kraina Serbs, who made up about 12 percent of the Croatia population. Many Serbs feared his outspoken hatred would generate a fascist regime, one in which Tudjman would use genocide to rid Croatia of any Serbs who remained there. Milosevic preached that the Serbs had every right to control their lands, even if the land was part of Croatia. With his nudging, Kraina Serbs grew restless.

In June 1991, Croatia and Slovenia seceded from the Yugoslav federation and declared independence. During the fight for secession, the Serb-dominated Yugoslav National Army (JNA) moved into Croatia to help the Kraina Serbs secure a quarter of the territory for themselves. UN special envoy Cyrus Vance worked out a cease-fire in January 1992, and UN peacekeepers arrived on the scene two months later to patrol the lines.

The battleground then moved to Bosnia, a region of mixed ethnic and religious backgrounds—40 percent Muslim, 32 percent Serb, and 18 percent Croat. Despite the diversity of its people, Bosnia had been known as a land of good feelings and harmony for many years. President Alija Izetbegovic was far from a Muslim extremist, but some of his enemies tried to paint him that way. Tudjman did not trust him and outwardly voiced his desire to see Bosnia divided between Serbia and Croatia. A fearful Izetbegovic begged UN peacekeepers for protection. American Ambassador Warren Zimmermann sent a cable to the U.S. government in Washington, D.C., backing up Izetbegovic's request. Washington brushed off the idea with the conventional belief that the proper time for peacekeepers was after a war, not before one.

Cyrus Vance and others urged Izetbegovic to hold off on declaring independence, fearing that such a move would prompt a war over control of Bosnia. Izetbegovic refused to listen, though, instead hoping that independence would bring him international recognition and the protection Bosnia so desperately needed. In February, Izetbegovic took a poll on the proposed secession. The referendum showed that Bosnian Muslims and Croats were in favor of secession, and they made up a 64 percent majority. The Serbs, however, boycotted the vote. When Izetbegovic declared independence, Milosevic and Bosnian Serb leader Radovan Karadzic accused Izetbegovic of forcing Serbs out of the Yugoslav federation against their will. With the obvious support of Milosevic and the Yugoslav army, Karadzic declared the Bosnian Serbs a republic, and the JNA launched an attack to put down the secession in April 1992. "You have to understand the Serbs, Mr. Zimmermann," Karadzic told the American ambassador. "They have been betrayed for centuries. Today they cannot live

Yugoslavia no more

Under the terms of an EU-sponsored plan to preserve their federation, Serbia and Montenegro will drop the name Yugoslavia.

Yugoslavia was a post–World War II federation that included the six countries of Slovenia, Croatia, Macedonia, Montenegro, Serbia, and Bosnia and Herzegovina (commonly shortened to just "Bosnia"). The map above shows how the federation was divided once more in the early 1990s.

with other nations. They must have their own separate existence. They are a warrior race, and they can trust only themselves to take by force what is their due."[38] After two months, the JNA withdrew, but left behind enough troops and weaponry to create a new Serb army in Bosnia. The Bosnian war had begun.

THE DESPERATE TIDE IN BOSNIA

The war in Bosnia took a gory and horrifying road. The Bosnian Serb army fought to create links between Bosnia and Serbia and Croatia. Conquered areas became breeding grounds of racism and genocide. Serbs worked to get rid of Muslims and Croats using a policy of "ethnic cleansing." Soldiers began by destroying mosques and non-Serb churches and homes. Then they terrorized the towns with looting, random killings, and rape. After devastating a conquered region, they herded the survivors off to prison camps, where they were further tortured, abused, and murdered.

The Serb soldiers laid siege to Sarajevo, once a beautiful and proud city boasting a half-million residents. Sarajevo had hosted the 1984 winter Olympics just eight years earlier. Now, it was scene of chaos. By the end of 1992, the Serbs controlled 70 percent of Bosnia. By November 1993, 10,000 Bosnians were dead in Sarajevo alone, 1,500 of them children. Worse still, there was little doubt that those civilians in Sarajevo killed by sniper fire had been direct targets of besieging Serbs—a gross war crime according to international law. Once again, the media flooded the public with footage of dying children, bedraggled women, fleeing refugees, and ravaged towns. Once again, the world called on the United Nations for help in Bosnia's desperation.

Annan and the Security Council ordered peacekeepers to Bosnia to protect the Sarajevo airport and convoys of the UN High Commissioner for Refugees (UNHCR), which was carrying food and medicine to desperate towns. At first, Bosnians cheered the peacekeepers as saviors, but their tears of joy quickly turned to disappointment and frustration. The peacekeepers only had authority to defend themselves and convoys—not to fight back at the Serbs. Nothing was done to put down the aggressors.

Reporters and critics took jabs at the United Nations' efforts in Bosnia, heralding that food gives little comfort to the suffering people of Sarajevo when they have to dodge bullets just to get it. Annan, who was juggling Somalia and Bosnia at the same time, felt backed up against a wall. The United States was quick to criticize the UN but slow to offer any suggestions or support. "I think we have to be careful not to blame the wrong people for the lack of collective will," Annan cautioned during a news conference in New York in November 1994. He continued,

Peacekeepers are usually the first on the ground, and the last to leave, and the first to be criticized. Quite frankly, the decisions have to be made by the capitals and the Security Council and not by the peacekeepers on the ground. . . . I think where we are presumed to have failed is when we are judged by unrealistic expectations. If we are expected to play the role as enforcers when we don't have the mandate and the resources, then we have failed.[39]

In other words, Annan stressed that the failure lies in governments who refuse to offer their support, not in the peacekeepers who are doing the best with what they have.

NATO DOES "NADA"

In early January 1993, UN hopes in the Bosnian conflict rose momentarily. Cyrus Vance and the British foreign secretary, David Owen, drew up a peace plan for the warring factions. The proposal divided Bosnia into 10 provinces—three Muslim, three Serbian, three Croat, and the tenth, Sarajevo, jointly governed by all three groups. The strategy was to sign up Bosian Croats and Muslims quickly, then apply international pressure to the Serbs and force them to sign.

Much to the astonishment of Vance and Owen, the plan backfired. At first, the Croats refused to sign. The Muslim government immediately trashed it, assuming that the United States' new president, Bill Clinton, would come up with something better. The truth was a disappointing blow for Bosnia—the United States did not pull through as hoped.

After deliberating on the plan for a month, President Clinton decided that the United States would engage in negotiations and back the plan. Valuable time was wasted, though, and the plan for peace had already lost its momentum. Under American pressure, the Muslims eventually signed the proposal, as the Croats already had. A flicker of promise was shown by Karadizic, who made a motion to sign. The plan was voted down in a Bosnian Serb referendum, however. It was back to square one for Kofi Annan and the UN Security Council. Many UN officials blamed the United States' hesitation for the unsuccessful outcome.

Trying to flex some muscle against the Serbian resistance, the UN called in the North Atlantic Treaty Organization (NATO). This alliance of 26 countries from North America and Europe was committed to preserving peace and security in the North Atlantic area. The Security Council imposed a "no-fly zone" in Bosnia, banning all military flights in Bosnian airspace. Unfortunately, the gesture turned out to be all talk. The council created no system of enforcing the zone. In March 1993, the Security Council finally passed a new resolution giving NATO jet fighters the authority to shoot down any plane or helicopter that violated the ban.

The resolution proved to be of little use. NATO fighters held back, in fear of a Serbian retaliation, and Serbs went about their business in defiance. One day in Sarajevo, as NATO planes roared overhead, a Bosnian journalist shouted, "What do they do for us? What are they here for? They don't help anyone."[40]

In 1995, the tide finally turned against the Serbs, when Croatian forces retook the region of Krajina in southeastern Croatia. The victory sent more than 170,000 Serbs fleeing in fear. After this devastating defeat, the three warring sides—now exhausted from fighting—agreed to hold cease-fire talks with the United Nations. In spite of pleas against a divided Bosnia, the Dayton Agreement of November 1995 separated Bosnia between a Serbian-controlled region and a Bosnian Federation of Croats and Muslims. In effect, the agreement rewarded the Serbian aggressors and left a teetering Bosnia.

Although the mission to Bosnia finished unhappily and left many UN officials unsatisfied, it did not end in total failure. Peacekeepers were able to deter major attacks on patrolled towns; in doing so, they lowered casualties and improved basic humanitarian conditions. Even in safe areas, however, living conditions were abhorrent—overcrowding, crime, and unemployment were rampant. Most unsettling was the uncertain future.

Fifty Years of Peacekeeping

Anniversaries are typically a time for reflection and appraisal, so no one doubted the UN would come under scrutiny in 1995, when it turned 50. Memories of the horrors of Somalia, Rwanda, and Bosnia still plagued the world. When the celebrations were planned two years in advance, however, everyone listened to proposals for reforms in the years ahead and assumed the general mood would be upbeat. Few anticipated the overall frustration and downheartedness that would prevail at the UN's 50-year mark.

For the previous 50 years, the UN certainly played a significant role in the world's affairs. An uneasiness pervaded the organization's staff, however. Over the years, whenever anything went awry in the world, UN officials were the scapegoats. Although most Americans still held the United Nations in high regard, public confidence was steadily eroding. Some U.S. officials were scornful of the UN. Although the UN is an international organization, it was hard to ignore American criticism with the UN headquarters towering over the East River in New York City.

Mostly, American disapproval stemmed from frustration at the failed peacekeeping missions in Somalia and Bosnia. The Republicans—who took control of both the Senate and the House of Representatives in 1994—proposed legislation that would halt any president who tried to send American troops into peacekeeping missions. More devastating, Congress worked to drastically reduce the amount of money the United States would allocate each year to peacekeeping efforts.

The United States was the UN's most important member state. If the United States decided to withdraw its interest in the UN, the organization would be left with few resources. The problem the UN faced in working with the United States—the richest and most powerful member state—was that it is hard to coax a great power to do things it does not want to do. For that reason, the UN was lucky to have Kofi Annan as secretary-general. He was able to persuade the United States to be more active.

Annan humbly acknowledged the UN's failings, and called on all human beings to pick up a torch to help the UN succeed. "The world cannot claim ignorance of what those who live here have endured," Annan said in Sarajevo in 1995.

> In looking back, we should all recall how we responded to the escalating horrors of the last four years. And, as we do, there are questions which each of us must ask: What did I do? Could I have done more? Did I let my prejudice, or my fear, overwhelm my reasoning? And above all, how would I react next time?[41]

Throughout his duties as assistant secretary-general for peacekeeping, Annan was learning about conflict. He discovered that peacekeeping tasks involve more than just ending wars and offering money. "To be a good mediator, you have to be a good listener," Annan later explained.

> To be able to help people, you have to listen to understand what their concerns are. I may walk into a situation and tell the people if you stop fighting, if you stop doing this or that, I will make sure you get economic assistance, you get financial assistance. That may not be their concern at all. Their concern may be fear—fear that if something is not done, the other group may eliminate them. Their very existence might be at risk. You need to understand that.[42]

No doubt, Annan cast a sympathetic eye to the people of Bosnia, who owned those exact fears.

CHAPTER 7

More Than Just a Job— A Calling

In 1996, Boutros Bourtros-Ghali's term as UN secretary-general was coming to a close. Throughout the halls of the United Nations, Kofi Annan's name was whispered as a potential candidate for replacement. Annan had never dreamed of being secretary-general. In fact, he did not think it was even possible. Up until this time, member states had always gone outside the organization to find a secretary-general. Besides, Annan never thought he would be with the United Nations even this long. He planned to work for just two years and then return home to Ghana.

When asked in 1996 whether he wanted to be secretary-general, Annan was undecided. Such a post would mean less privacy for Nane and him. "If it's to come to me, it will," he answered. "If not, it won't."[43] Some critics thought Annan was too soft spoken and not tough enough for the demanding leadership role of secretary-general. Others heralded him for "his efficiency, his exquisite tact and his slightly mysterious powers of persuasion."[44] So, after several vetoes from the French—who championed Boutros-Ghali—the Security Council

Kofi Annan, facing the camera, embraces Ismail Razali, president of the UN General Assembly, after taking the oath of office as secretary-general in December 1996.

finally agreed to nominate Annan. A few days later, the General Assembly elected the 57-year-old as the seventh UN secretary-general—the first to come from within UN ranks.

After his election, Annan and Nane moved from their home in Roosevelt Island to a UN-owned mansion on Sutton Place, a neighborhood on Manhattan's East Side. The house—which has a lovely view of the East River—is within walking distance of UN Headquarters. Promotion to the UN's top post did offer Annan a nice raise—a yearly salary of $227,253—which still is modest compared to the responsibilities he holds. By comparison, current U.S. President George W. Bush earns $400,000 a year. As Annan puts it, "No one joins the Secretariat to become rich and famous."[45]

Annan moved into the United Nations' top job at a difficult time. The past five years had been marred with failure. Around the world, the UN was resented. America held the biggest grudge—owing more than one billion dollars in dues and refusing to pay up if changes were not made. On his first day, Annan commented, "It is like the first day of school. Everyone expects a lot from you and you get into it with considerable trepidation."[46] Nevertheless, Annan was determined to win back the world's trust and support. He believed that service in the United Nations was more than just a job—it was a calling. "The member states have made it clear that they want changes and they have given us unanimous support," Annan said.

> I think together we can achieve a lot, bring about the reforms that are necessary, encourage the member states to work together, to honor the commitment to the organization, and together make the changes that are required if we are to make the United Nations as relevant as it ought to be as we move into the twenty-first century.[47]

His optimism brought with it a host of reforms.

Within months of taking office in 1997, Annan announced the first phase of his reform program: to repair the UN's image and facilitate payment of overdue UN membership fees by the United States. Annan's proposal included the elimination of 1,000 jobs from the Secretariat, cutting administrative costs of the Secretariat from 38 percent to 25 percent of the budget, and overhauling the Department of Public Information, which was often criticized for its poor communications strategy.

In July 1997, he announced phase two—the consolidation of many programs, aimed at reducing overlap and improving accountability. He created a Senior Management Group to oversee various sections of the United Nations—peace and security, humanitarian affairs, development and economic and social affairs. In addition, Annan added the post of deputy secretary-general, to improve management and guide inter-departmental work.

By carrying out these reforms, Annan was able to persuade the United States to pay back a portion of its debt. Critics complained that Annan hadn't done enough to make a real impact. For example, the 1,000 jobs cut were positions that were not actually occupied. In addition, combining like programs was more likely to affect efficiency than the budget. Annan was making a move toward a more adept, less fumbling United Nations, however.

Until he accepted his new post, Annan's work throughout the world came as a direct result of conflict and war. As secretary-general, he hoped to change the world from a more positive angle—through prevention. Annan's theory of prevention is a practical one: It saves money and it saves lives. Annan's idea was not necessarily a new one—he revived an old principle first introduced by the UN's second secretary-general, Dag Hammarskjöld. Like Hammarskjöld, Annan believed the best way to keep peace is before fighting breaks out—not in a reaction to it. Prevention, he proposes, also applies to nonmilitary disasters.

Humans will always face natural hazards—flood, droughts, violent storms, and earthquakes—but many of today's disasters are manmade. Poverty and population push people to live directly in the path of harm—on floodplains, earthquake zones, or precarious hillsides. Massive logging operations reduce the soil's ability to absorb rainfall, which contributes to erosion and flooding.

In an effort to prevent tragedy, Annan assigned United Nations agencies to be in charge of natural prevention. The Food and Agriculture Organization (FAO) provides vital warnings of impending famines, and the World Meteorological Organization helps to forecast cyclones and droughts. In addition, Annan began putting pressure on governments to enforce stricter codes on construction work, avoiding areas vulnerable to natural disaster. Annan's programs of prevention are not just a stab in the dark—they are based on programs that have worked. For example, over the years China implemented disaster-prevention efforts to reduce flooding tragedies. Massive flooding in 1931 claimed the lives of more than 140,000 people. Another flood in 1954 took 33,000 lives. By 1998, when the flood waters rose again, that number was reduced to 3,000 lives.

Preventing war is much more complex, but there is no higher goal or deeper commitment of the United Nations. The United Nations uses the same tactics it has for years: preventive diplomacy, preventive deployment, and preventive disarmament. Preventive diplomacy is peacekeeping through mediation, conciliation, or negotiation. It is quiet, low-key, and noninvasive. The next step, preventive deployment, is the "thin blue line" in avoiding conflict by building confidence in areas of tension. Preventive disarmament—the trickiest of the three—attempts to reduce the number of weapons in a conflict-prone zone, thus ensuring peace. At times, preventive disarmament includes the collection of small arms. These weapons do not cause wars, but they can facilitate the dramatic increase of a war's deadlines and duration.

In conflict-prone areas, a long-term prevention strategy is often necessary. Annan acknowledged that in these cases, the United Nations must address the root causes of conflict, which often center around power, wealth, or ethnic and religious differences. In time, Annan hopes the UN can find ways to forge peace agreements before destructive wars arise. As the history of the United Nations proves, prevention requires action and international unity. Annan admits, "While the genocide in Rwanda will define for our generation the consequences of inaction in the face of mass murder, the more recent conflict in Kosovo has prompted important questions about the consequences of action in the absence of complete unity on the part of the international community."[48]

Providing humanitarian aid is one of the UN's topmost priorities. The problem is, the international community does not react to humanitarian needs and emergencies in a consistent way. The media play a leading role in how aid is distributed. For example, the crisis in Kosovo received saturated coverage, whereas a more deadly war between Eritrea and Ethiopia received very little. Still other wars went on with almost no coverage at all. "It is my strong view that such assistance should not be allocated on the basis of media coverage, politics or geography," Annan states. "Its sole criterion should be human need."[49]

Annan did not stop there. Later in his term, as the new millennium approached, Annan saw an opportunity to raise the bar on how the United Nations touches the world. He set eight Millennium Development Goals, or MDGs. The MDGs proposed by Annan range from cutting extreme poverty in half to ending the spread of HIV/AIDS and providing primary education around the world—and all by 2015. Annan understands the work needed to reach such aggressive goals, but he believes in the dedication of the United Nations. "We cannot win overnight," Annan explained. "Success will require sustained action across the entire decade between now and the deadline. It takes time to train the teachers, nurses and engineers; to build the roads, schools and hospitals; to grow the small and large businesses able to create the jobs and income needed. So we must start now."[50] The eight goals are as follows:

1. Eradicate extreme poverty and hunger.
2. Achieve universal primary education.

3. Promote gender equality and empower women.
4. Reduce child mortality.
5. Improve maternal health.
6. Combat HIV/AIDS, malaria, and other diseases.
7. Ensure environmental sustainability.
8. Develop a global partnership for development—create a blueprint agreed on by all member states for trading, finances, technology, debt relief, affordable drugs, and others.

With the bureaucracy in better check, Annan's negotiation skills were about to be put to the ultimate test.

Responsibility of the World

The role of UN secretary-general is to be responsible for the world, without having the authority to govern it. When someone once asked Kofi Annan if he had power, he responded, "I do not have any armies, nor any resources at my disposal. But I have a blip of it. I try to speak for the weak, the poor, and the voiceless. I try to encourage governments and ask them to help on their behalf."* As secretary-general, Annan is chief administrator of the United Nations and head of the UN Secretariat, with its 50,000 international civil service officers. Annan oversees hundreds of programs, funds, and agencies, and in his minimal spare time, he balances the budget. In addition to his formal duties, Annan is expected to uphold the values of the United Nations and to act as its moral authority—a job that requires a strong character.

In theory, the secretary-general should have a hefty resume. According to the founders of the United Nations, the best secretary-general would have a great deal of diplomatic and political experience. More important, he or she must know when to be dynamic and forceful and when to back off. In reality, however, when it comes time to appoint a secretary-general, politics carries more weight than qualifications, leadership skills, and personality.

SADDAM HUSSEIN'S LAST CHANCE

The Persian Gulf War in 1991 left plenty of unfinished business in the eyes of many countries, especially the United States. All hopes that Saddam Hussein might be overthrown in a military coup after the war quickly evaporated, and the world was left wondering what Hussein might do next. There seemed to be no limit to the dictator's ambitions. The embargo on Iraq's commercial exports—including oil—was still in effect, until Iraq agreed to the Security Council's conditions. At the end of the war, one major objective of the United Nations was to eliminate Iraq's weapons of mass destruction—nuclear, biological, or chemical weapons

The United Nations will often bend an ear to the United States—the wealthiest and most powerful member state—when it considers candidates for the position.

Typically, the post of secretary-general rotates after two five-year terms, so that the position can be held by someone from another area of the world. UN member states usually belong to one of five regions—Africa, Asia, Latin America and the Caribbean, Eastern Europe, and Western Europe. Annan, who succeeded Boutros Boutros-Ghali of Egypt, was reelected in 2001, even though a representative of Africa had already held the seat for two terms. Because Annan was so popular among the member states and UN staff, the Asian states—who were up for the post—did not challenge the reelection.

With the globe as his jurisdiction, Annan jets from country to country on a regular basis. Surprisingly, he does not have his own plane but rather travels on commercial airlines. If a commercial flight is not available, a member state will usually provide a private plane. Even this gesture is not free, however—the expenses incurred are subtracted from that country's membership dues.

---

*"Nikita Khrushchev," Wikipedia.
  Available at http://en.wikipedia.org/wiki/Nikita_Khrushchev.

and ballistic missiles with a range of more than 100 miles. In order to do this, the Security Council established the UN Special Commission (UNSCOM) on Iraq. The objective of UNSCOM was not only for UN inspectors to find and destroy weapons of mass destruction, but also for the inspectors to be permitted to continue monitoring the situation, to ensure that Iraq would not reacquire banned weapons. There was no telling what kinds of weapons Hussein harbored or was creating, though—not until he would allow UN inspectors to check it out.

A wisp of hope arose in November 1994, when Annan was still assistant secretary-general of peacekeeping: Hussein officially recognized the sovereignty of Kuwait and accepted the border between the two nations. Back at UN Headquarters, the Security Council debated whether this act was enough of a reason to lift sanctions on Iraq. All 15 council nations had insisted on Iraq's acceptance of Kuwaiti independence as one condition for lifting the ban on commercial exports. Russia pledged to work in the Security Council to lift the oil embargo if Iraq relinquished its claims to Kuwait and agreed to cooperate with the UNSCOM team. If Hussein agreed to these terms, Russia would offer economic aid to Iraq's wobbling economy.

In April 1995, the UN Security Council passed a resolution allowing a partial lift of oil sanctions to buy food and medicine for the Iraqi people. Later, this exception would become known as the "Oil-for-Food Program." Reluctantly, Hussein accepted the offer. Saddam Hussein's facade of cooperation quickly disappeared, however. At the end of the summer, he attempted to shake loose the ropes of his confinement. Defying U.S. warnings, Hussein ordered 30,000 soldiers into a northern Kurdish stronghold and stomped over the city of Irbil. Without missing a stride, he further pushed his forces into an Iraqi region home to 3.5 million Kurds, an area that American-led forces had promised to protect. The United States saw this invasion as a direct violation of UN Resolution 688, which forbade Hussein from suppressing the Kurds and demanded that he respect the human and political rights of all his citizens. In September, U.S. warships fired on Iraqi air defenses in southern Iraq. Hussein retaliated with return fire, but held back from unleashing an all-out war. For the next two years, Hussein toyed with his enemies, instigating occasional skirmishes with U.S. and British fighters. Hussein, however, was far from foolish. He knew he would lose a military face-off with the United Nations, so he opted for a different tactic—a game of cat-and-mouse with UN weapons inspectors.

From the very beginning of the weapons inspections, Hussein dug in his heels. Only three weeks into the program, a UNSCOM team attempted to stop Iraqi vehicles carrying nuclear-related equipment. When inspectors tried to approach the vehicles, Iraqi transporters fired warning shots into the air to keep them away. Every few months between the cease-fire and 1997, UN investigators reported holes and inconsistencies, false information, and numerous attempts to deliberately mislead UN inspectors. All the while, Iraq insisted it was complying with inspections.

By 1994, UNSCOM teams had accounted for most of Iraq's nuclear and missile holds, but they still knew little about Hussein's chemical and biological weapons. Ingredients needed to create chemical weapons, which kill victims by exposing them to poisonous gases, are relatively easy to identify. Biological weapons, however, inflict death through the spread of infectious diseases, and these organisms are inexpensive to make with basic equipment. A factory that is supposedly making yeast for bread could be a clandestine operation growing bacteria for anthrax. In fact, this concern is what prompted the inspection of the Al-Hakam protein plant southwest of Baghdad.

The clue that tipped investigators was the plant's enormous size. Great amounts of protein can be grown in small spaces, so there should be no reason to have such a large facility. The maze of pipes, heating units, conveyors, and funnels raised questions with UNSCOM teams. When inspectors uncovered rows of steel drums containing a growth medium powder, their suspicions were confirmed. Growth medium is needed to make protein, but it is also necessary to produce biological weapons. For its purposes, Iraq should need only about one ton of growth medium per year. The steel drums, however, held 34 tons. UNSCOM members deduced that the Al-Hakam plant was manufacturing anthrax—a deadly organism that can kill a human being in 48 hours. Inspectors immediately destroyed the plant, but what else was Hussein hiding, and where?

When boxes of top-secret Iraqi documents turned up on a Baghdad chicken farm in 1995, UN frustrations intensified. Until then, Hussein had insisted he had no such documents. In 1997, UNSCOM became more aggressive in its search for biological weapons. New teams of spies followed suspicious Iraqis to potential hiding places for weapons. These undercover missions stiffened Iraqi resistance. In November, Hussein expelled six members of the UNSCOM team, and by December, inspections had ground to a halt. With the United States losing patience and anxious to take military action, Annan had to make a last-ditch effort to maintain peace.

In February 1998, Annan hopped a plane to Baghdad—as always, with a positive outlook—hoping that he could do business with Saddam Hussein. He met the Iraqi leader at one of the palaces and sat down to negotiations. In a light-hearted yet awkward atmosphere, they joked back and forth. Then Hussein's rhetoric took a dark and winding journey through the suffering of his people, and how the world had been so unfair to him. After about an hour, Hussein's officials and Annan's group left the room—leaving the two leaders alone. Hussein stated that he simply would not accept opening the palaces indefinitely, but he was willing to open them for inspections. He stood by the explanation that it was not only a matter of national dignity, but of security. His officials live and work in the palaces, and he did not want classified information slipping into the hands of passersby.

"This is not going to work," Annan firmly replied. "I'm here with the unanimous decision of the Council that you have to open up everything, including the palaces. And that we will have to

Former Iraqi President Saddam Hussein is shown here at a meeting of the Revolution Command Council and the Ba'ath Party Command in February 1997. At this meeting, the groups issued a statement that condemned the UN Security Council's latest resolution threatening further sanctions on Iraq unless it cooperated with UN weapons inspectors.

reserve the right to come back and that there should be no time limit." After two hours of negotiating, Annan finally got Hussein to agree to those terms. Annan explained that failure to comply would be a tragedy; the United States and its allies would surely take action. "I'm here to give you a chance to resolve this," Annan said, "and this is really the last chance."[51] In the end, Hussein agreed, but added, "The language has to respect our dignity."[52]

Many people criticized the UN for even attempting negotiations. If anything came out of the talks, it would certainly be in Hussein's favor and ultimately water down UNSCOM's efforts. Nevertheless, Annan exited the talks with optimism. He had convinced Hussein to open palaces that nobody had gone into for seven years. This breakthrough could only strengthen inspections. He also understood the importance of enforcing the agreements, though. "We should all hold him up to the promises he had made," Annan said. "The proof of the pudding is in the eating. He has to demonstrate that he will deliver. If he doesn't, he knows the consequences."[53]

Unfortunately, the secretary-general's last-minute accord disintegrated eight months later. On October 31, 1998, Iraq ended all cooperation with UNSCOM. Hussein's blatant disregard for UN resolutions divided the Security Council on what to do. Tired of trying to get Iraq to comply with the United Nations, France, Russia, and China voted to end sanctions in an effort to save what was left of Iraq's economy. The United States and Britain threatened to veto the move—fearing that Hussein would never learn his lesson. Before a UN showdown, however, the United States ended the debate with an attack on Iraq. The strike had lukewarm approval from the Security Council, because the United States had still left a door open for a diplomatic solution by supporting the oil-for-food program. Iraq could continue to sell oil at market prices under UN contracts. Funds from the sales were put into an escrow account and used to import food, medicine, and other humanitarian supplies. Annan redoubled his efforts to find a way to end the conflict before it exploded into war, but Hussein's radical support for extremist groups would soon awaken a sleeping bear.

TROUBLE IN KOSOVO

Iraq was just one issue on Annan's mind; trouble loomed in other parts of the world, as well. After the dissection of Bosnia in 1995, attention shifted to the Yugoslav province of Kosovo in Serbia, which had been in turmoil for several years. The province was primarily Albanian, but it was ruled by the Serb minority and

Milosevic in Belgrade. By 1993, 400,000 Albanians had already left Kosovo because of deteriorating socioeconomic conditions. Many Albanians also bitterly opposed the internationally-supervised Dayton Agreement, which failed to recognize their long-standing demand for independence by forbidding further border changes in Yugoslavia. With tension mounting between Serbs and Albanians, both sides began arming themselves.

In March 1997, the civil government in Kosovo collapsed into anarchy. As civil war heated up, Western Europe and the United States became increasingly concerned about the possibility of another Bosnia ordeal. The United States blamed Milosevic for the violence, and in October 1998, NATO gained authorization to launch air strikes if Milosevic failed to comply with UN Security Council demands—to end violence in Kosovo and allow Albanian refugees to return home. Under the threat of an American-backed war, Milosevic withdrew the bulk of his Serbian military forces and permitted NATO fly-overs and UN observers in Kosovo.

This show of peace was short-lived. Interpreting the demands as NATO standing on their side, Albanians intensified their military efforts. Serbs responded by once again mounting their army. A battle ensued, and the Serbian army crushed the Kosovo Liberation Army, bringing an end to the October peace agreement. By January 1999, NATO was once again prepared to use military force to end the fighting.

The imminent military strike sparked negotiations in Rambouillet, near Paris, in mid March. The peace agreement primarily consisted of several key points: (1) an immediate and verifiable end of violence and repression in Kosovo; (2) deployment of international civil and security presences, endorsed and adopted by the United Nations; and (3) the safe return of all refugees to their homes. At the end of the talks, the Kosovar Albanian delegation signed the peace agreement, but the Serbs did not. Milosevic accused the United Nations of supporting the Albanian side. If he agreed to allow the United Nations to set up an interim government, Milosevic believed it would ultimately mean the severing of Kosovo from Serbia. He could not have that.

When U.S. Special Envoy Richard Holbrooke asked Milosevic if he understood what would happen if he refused to sign the Rambouillet Accord, Milosevic replied, "You are going to bomb us." Holbrooke responded, "That's right."[54] There was no misunderstanding. Bombing began on March 24.

After 77 days of air strikes, Milosevic and the Federal Republic of Yugoslavia agreed to withdraw all Yugoslav forces from Kosovo. The NATO secretary-general immediately wrote Annan and the UN Security Council, informing them of the development. The UN Security Council passed a resolution outlining the demands of the Rambouillet Accord, bringing an end to the Kosovo crisis. But years of war had ravaged Kosovo and its economy. Bringing the refugees home would be a daunting task—many of their homes now lie in ashes.

In September 2000, Milosevic—still claiming power—finally agreed to hold a presidential election. Much to his surprise, the people elected Socialist Vojislav Kostunica. At first, Milosevic refused to acknowledge Kostunica's sweeping victory. When the streets filled with protestors, however, he at last stepped down.

Although the UN was not allowed to be a prominent player in the Kosovo crisis, Annan understood its importance in the peace-keeping mission that followed the war and the enormous humanitarian efforts that followed. As he has often commented, "We never start it, but we often have to finish it and clean it up."[55]

CHAPTER 8

Peace Has No Parade

The secretary-general's graceful diplomacy and soft-spoken manner won the admiration and loyalty of the Secretariat, UN staff, civil service workers, and political leaders abroad. On June 29, 2001, the General Assembly elected Annan to serve a second term, even though the African continent had already held the seat for two terms. According to general rule, another area of the world should take a turn to be represented. With Annan's overwhelming popularity, however, no one challenged the decision.

In the early morning hours of October 12, 2001, a ring of the telephone startled Annan out of bed. The voice on the other end was his spokesperson, Fred Eckhard. In Annan's business, an early-morning phone call usually meant something disastrous. He braced himself for the worst. Much to his surprise, Eckhard had wonderful news—Annan and the United Nations had been jointly awarded the Nobel Peace Prize. Eckhard had called to congratulate him. Annan felt humbled by the honor, but also encouraged. It was clear that the Nobel Committee recognized the challenges the United Nations faces each and every day. Although there have been both successes and failures, the Committee obviously believed the United Nations could rise to new challenges and make the world a happier, more peaceful place in which to live.

In December, Annan and Nane flew to Oslo, Norway, where Annan would be presented with the prize. On his arrival, he held a press conference. One reporter asked Annan if he was uneasy about accepting the Nobel Peace Prize when there were so many conflicts around the world. Annan replied,

> You are right. That seems rather off to be receiving the peace prize at a time when we have so many conflicts. But I think that also exemplifies the world we live in—the good and evil unfortunately live side by side. What is important is that we do not lose hope, and we have the courage to keep working to end conflict.[56]

Even on such a celebratory trip, Annan still had work to do as secretary-general. On one morning of his stay, Annan, the General Assembly president, and their wives were joined by the Crown Princess of Norway in an open-air event at the seaside near Oslo's City Hall. There, thousands of schoolchildren cheered the Nobel Laureates. Annan made a brief speech, telling the children that they were the leaders of the twenty-first century. Annan also made an appearance at the Oslo synagogue for a ceremony to light the first candles of Hanukkah. Afterward, he met with family members of three Israeli soldiers and a businessman who were abducted in late 2000 by the Lebanese terrorist group Hezbollah. The families expressed gratitude to Annan for his efforts to gather information on their whereabouts and safety. With tears in their eyes, they urged him to push for the return of any still living and for the bodies of the dead. Annan assured them that he would do all he could to bring them closure.

At the award ceremony, with the blare of trumpets, Annan stepped up to accept the Nobel Peace Prize. In his acceptance address, Annan eloquently spoke of peace and security being the

Kofi Annan is pictured here shortly after receiving the Nobel Peace Prize on December 10, 2001. The prize that year was awarded jointly to Annan and the United Nations. South Korean Foreign Minister Han Seung-soo (right), also the president of the UN General Assembly, accepted the award on behalf of the organization.

rights of every member of the human race. He stressed the need for the international community to work together to protect these rights for others. "What begins with the failure to uphold the dignity of one life, all too often ends with a calamity for entire nations," he said. He warned that genocide begins with the killing of a single man, "not for what he has done, but because of who he is."[57]

In the new century, Annan called for the understanding that peace not only belongs to states, but to every member within those communities: "The sovereignty of States must no longer be used as a shield for gross violations of human rights," he declared.[58] The recognition of the United Nations as a champion of human rights—and symbol of international unity—is one step closer to global peace.

Annan acknowledged that in a world filled with weapons and war, a prize for peace is rare. Nations around the world have bronze statues of battle heroes and war memorials. "But peace has no parade," he reminded his audience, "no pantheon of victory."[59]

Even though Annan accepted the award, the Nobel Peace Prize belonged to both the world body and its leader. Annan acknowledged everyone's contributions as integral to the function and success of the United Nations. Shortly after receiving news of the award, Annan addressed his staff, "This is an indispensable Organization, but an Organization that can only work because of the staff and your dedication."[60] The UN civil service workers are often on the front lines, and yet they are prepared to travel to any corner of the world in service of peace. "Today that work has been recognized," Annan applauded. "I hope it will urge us forward and encourage all of us to tackle our tasks with even greater determination."[61]

Over the years, the UN system has been awarded the Nobel Peace Prize on five other occasions. The award was given to the Office of the United Nations High Commissioner for Refugees (UNHCR) in both 1954 and 1981, whereas the United Nations

Children's Fund (UNICEF) received the prize in 1965 and the International Labour Organization (ILO) in 1969. The UN Peacekeeping Operations accepted the award in 1988. Annan is the second secretary-general to receive the Nobel Peace Prize. The UN's second secretary-general, Dag Hammarskjöld, was awarded the prize shortly after his death in 1961, for his work in strengthening the United Nations.

PLIGHT OF A WAR-TORN COUNTRY: AFGHANISTAN

Just a month before Annan took his glorious phone call from Fred Eckhard, the world was shaken by tragedy. On September 11, 2001, terrorists flying two passenger jets crashed into the Twin Towers of the World Trade Center in New York City. About an hour later, another plane spiraled into the Pentagon in Arlington, Virginia. Yet another plane crashed in a field in Somerset County, Pennsylvania, southeast of Pittsburgh. The devastation that day took nearly 3,000 lives. Al Qaeda, a terrorist group led by extremist Osama bin Laden, claimed responsibility for the attacks. In response, the United States initiated military action against Taliban-led Afghanistan, which had been accused of protecting bin Laden in the past.

On November 10, world leaders gathered at the UN headquarters as America began bombing Afghanistan in retaliation for the terrorist attacks. (At the time, Annan was also mired in 15 other conflicts.) Annan stepped up to the podium before a hushed assembly. "We meet nearly seven weeks later than we intended, and we all know why," Annan began. "No words can express our revulsion and sorrow on the senseless loss of life on 11 September. The United Nations is indeed the indispensable common house of the human family. When the family is under attack, it is under the common house that its members gather to decide what to do."[62]

Afghanistan had been mired in conflict for many years. Beginning in late 1994, a militia of Pashtun Islamic fundamentalists—the Taliban—emerged as a growing and powerful force in the country. In early 1996, as the Taliban continued to gain control, the group captured Kabul, the capital city, and declared themselves the legitimate government of Afghanistan. The militia imposed repressive laws across the two-thirds of the country they controlled. The Taliban brutally violated the human rights of Afghan women, who were forced to be fully veiled and were forbidden from going to work, school, or out of the house alone.

By August 1998, the Taliban appeared on the verge of taking over the entire country. After terrorists bombed the U.S. embassies in Kenya and Tanzania, U.S. missiles destroyed what was believed to be a terrorist training camp near Kabul. The complex was thought to be run by Osama bin Laden, the militant mastermind accused of the embassy bombings.

In March 1999, the UN managed to forge a peace agreement between the Taliban and its enemies—the non-Pashtun forces of the Northern Alliance. The peace accord was short-lived, however, and fighting broke out several months later. For breaking the resolution, the United Nations imposed economic sanctions on Afghanistan in November. Because of this action, coupled with the U.S. missile attacks, Afghanis refused to turn bin Laden over to authorities. In 2000, additional UN sanctions were put into effect, including a ban on arm sales to Taliban forces.

Even with the sanctions, by 2000 the Taliban controlled nearly 90 percent of the country. Still, their government was not recognized by the international community. The UN recognized President Burhanuddin Rabbani and the Northern Alliance. Continued warfare caused more than a million deaths, and 3 million refugees fled to Pakistan and Iran. Adding to the nation's woes, a drought stretched its deadly fingers across Asia beginning in the late 1990s, the most severe part of it hitting Afghanistan. Earthquakes in 1998 and 1999 also caused great devastation to the country.

After the terrorist attacks on American soil, the United States demanded that Afghanis hand over bin Laden. When they refused, the United States launched air strikes, followed by a swift ground campaign. In early December 2001, a new interim leader was appointed in Afghanistan, Hamid Karzai replacing Rabbani. By January 2002, the Taliban and al Qaeda had been mostly defeated.

Like Annan said, the job of the UN is often to finish up and clean up what others have started. With the Taliban practically ousted, it was the UN's turn to help stabilize the new regime. On January 25, 2002, Annan arrived in Kabul. He fought his way through chaotic crowds to a UN vehicle. The UN officials rode through the city streets, past the crumbling ruins of buildings. Afghanis lined the nearly desolate roadsides, stretching their necks for a peek at the person they hoped would rescue them.

During talks with the Afghanis, Annan—who could not speak the language and needed an interpreter—carefully watched the face and the gestures of whomever was speaking. As secretary-general, he needed to deal with many different cultures and languages. Not all peoples are as direct as the Americans; they are sometimes very subtle. Annan has learned to look into their eyes and read their body language. "You must listen to not only what is being said," Annan explained, "but what is not said, which is often much more important than what they say."[63] Nobody has more credibility in Afghanistan than the United Nations, despite failed peace attempts and humanitarian efforts that have fallen short. Unlike many situations Annan finds himself thrust into, this government wants to work with him.

Afghanistan has the opportunity to start anew. According to Annan, this chance should not be missed by Afghanis, their neighbors, or the international community. But Annan fears that international support will not be there for these people. After September 11, nations swore, "never again." Never again would they abandon a country and risk such a horrific outcome. Many nations pledged to rebuild Afghanistan, but promises are much easier to muster than is handing over cash. The UN asked for $10 billion to aid Afghanis. The international community pledged $4.5 billion, and even prospects of seeing this amount looks grim.

History of the Nobel Peace Prize

The Nobel Prize is an international award given each year since 1901 for achievements in physics, chemistry, physiology, medicine, literature, and working toward peace. The man behind this innovative prize was Alfred Nobel, born in 1833 in Stockholm, Sweden. Nobel's family were descendants of Olof Rudbeck, the best-known technical genius in Sweden during the 1600s. A chemist and engineer, Nobel invented dynamite in 1866. Later, he built dynamite companies and explosive-testing laboratories in more than 20 countries all over the world. Although lesser known, Nobel was also a playwright, but only of one play called *Nemesis.*

On November 27, 1895, Nobel wrote his last will. In it he established the Nobel Prize. In the will, he stated, "The whole of my remaining realizable estate shall be dealt with in the following way: The capital, invested in safe securities by my executors, shall constitute a fund, the interest on which shall be annually distributed in the form of prizes to those who, during the preceding year, shall have conferred the greatest benefit to mankind."* Nobel died of a cerebral hemorrhage on December 10, 1896, in his home in San Remo, Italy.

There are many ways to achieve peace in the world, and the Peace Prize can take countless avenues. Aside from humanitarian work and peace movements, the prize can be awarded for mediating international conflicts, advocating for human rights, and working toward disarmament. The first prize, awarded in 1901, was shared by Henry Dunant, founder of the Red Cross, and Frédéric Passy, an international pacifist leader of the time. Probably a source of great pride and satisfaction for Annan, Nelson Mandela and Frederik Willem de Klerk shared the prize in 1993 for their peaceful termination of the apartheid regime and for laying the foundations for a new democracy in South Africa. On the centennial anniversary of the prize in 2001, Kofi Annan and the United Nations received the award for helping to create a better organized and more peaceful world.

---

*"Excerpt from the Will of Alfred Nobel," NobelPrize.org. Available at http://nobelprize.org/nobel/alfred-nobel/biographical/will/index.html.

Currently, the UN has a peacekeeping force in Kabul, trying day and night to restore peace and security to that beaten city. The United States and other Western countries refuse to increase that peacekeeping force so that it can spread to the surrounding countryside. Meanwhile, the UN is stuck in the middle, working to rebuild a tattered country without adequate resources. Annan admits that if the international community refuses to take interest in an area for one reason or another, there is very little the UN can do. The secretary-general does not have the authority, unless he is backed up with money, personnel, and, occasionally, force. At least for now—after 20 years—the war in Afghanistan has been stopped, however.

The UN helps in any way it is able. For six years, the Taliban denied Afghani girls an education. In a UN-sponsored program, girls are attending school—many of them for the first time. When Annan visited the school, a handful of girls held up paper signs with the word "peace" written in both English and Afghani. Annan smiled and commented, "I see everyone wants peace."[64]

A rocky, difficult path stretches before the people of Afghanistan. Annan commented to one of the ministers, "What a job—to rebuild this nation." The minister poignantly replied, "Reconstruction can be done. Houses, roads, we can build. But the Afghani spirit is broken. How do you put that together?"[65] As he stated in his Nobel address, Annan hopes the nations of the world will unite to help each other—including Afghanistan—through difficult times.

CHAPTER 9

Oil for Food —Whose Scandal?

I n November 2003, Annan handed over the UN Oil-for-Food (OFF) Program—together with remaining funds and assets—to the Coalition Provisional Authority of Iraq. The program was one of the largest, most complex, and strangest tasks ever entrusted to the Secretariat—the only humanitarian program ever funded entirely from resources belonging to the nation it was designed to help.

After the Iraqi invasion of Kuwait in August 1990, the UN Security Council closed the doors on Iraq's exports and imports. At that time, no one imagined the sanctions would stay intact for nearly 13 years, or the devastating toll they would take on the health and nutrition of millions of innocent people. As early as 1991, the United Nations made its first proposition to Iraq, enabling the country to sell limited quantities of oil as income to meet its people's needs. Hussein refused the offer.

By 1995, with sanctions still in effect, Iraq's basic services—electricity, hospital care, education—had severely deteriorated. Still, Hussein made no move to comply with UN resolutions, compliance that would lift the sanctions. In an attempt to save the lives of innocent Iraqis, the Council drew up another resolution. Finally, in May 1995, the Iraqi government agreed to sign it. The first oil export under the Oil-for-Food Program was in December 1996, and the first shipments of food arrived, at last, in 1997.

Under the program, Annan was to supervise the sale of Iraqi oil and monitor the spending of proceeds. In its seven years of operation, the OFF Program had been expected to meet nearly impossible challenges, allocating $46 billion of export earnings on behalf of the Iraqi people. During its lifetime, nine different UN agencies and programs were created to manage humanitarian operations in Iraq in order to meet the needs of a civilian population that spanned some 24 economic and social districts. Over seven years, the program delivered enough food rations to sufficiently feed all 27 million Iraqi residents—cutting in half the rate of malnutrition in children. Between 1996 and 2001, caloric intake among Iraqis rose by 83 percent. During the same time period, enough medicines and vaccines were imported to eradicate polio and drastically reduce other, often deadly communicable diseases, including cholera, malaria, measles, mumps, tuberculosis, and meningitis. With such an impressive portfolio, it is hard to believe anything could taint its reputation. Nothing tarnishes a staff faster, however, than scandal.

SLINGING ALLEGATIONS

As early as 2000, UN overseers of the OFF program became suspicious of illegal oil surcharges the Iraqi government was placing on its exports. In order to get Hussein to comply with the resolution, the UN agreed to let him choose his business partners. This compromise may have been a mistake. After flagging dubious surcharges and suppliers, the UN Secretariat strengthened its contract review procedures, but it was later discovered that hands were still moving under the table. These "hands" helped Hussein pocket millions of dollars.

When the scandal was first discovered in 2004, press reports claimed Hussein had smuggled more than $20 billion from under the UN's nose. The U.S. Government Accountability Office (GAO) estimated that from 1997 to 2002, the former Iraqi regime acquired $10.1 billion in illegal revenues, including $5.7 billion in smuggled oil and $4.4 billion in surcharges on oil sales and unlawful commissions from suppliers exporting goods to Iraq through the OFF program. According to a report of the United States Central Intelligence Agency (CIA) Iraq Survey Group (ISG), these amounts were grossly exaggerated. Their findings revealed $1.74 billion of illicit revenue directly tied to the OFF program that could have been skimmed off in two ways.

First, there is evidence to suggest that Hussein deliberately underpriced his oil. Instead of the full monies going into the UN escrow account, a secret commission was demanded from the purchasers and not revealed to the UN, but either placed into secret accounts or pocketed by others to whom Hussein gave vouchers as political favors. In 2000, the UN oil overseers became aware of this practice and required Iraq to fix its prices. Hussein also persuaded companies in the program to overprice their food and other goods, then pay him back the difference in cash. This abuse was much more difficult for UN officials to detect.

News of the scandal stunned Annan, who had no idea what was going on within his organization, and it enraged many government officials. Members of the media and some government officials began slinging wild allegations. Some U.S. reporters even went so far as to suggest that Hussein used his illegal revenues to fund terrorist groups, particularly al Qaeda, and that the money is now in the hands of Iraqi insurgents—claims completely unproven. U.S. Senator Norm Coleman (R-Minn.), who is leading the congressional investigation into the program, advised Annan to resign, because "the scandal occurred on his watch." He went on to say, "I think there's a terrible stain on the credibility and the reputation of the United Nations, there's no doubt about that. If we're ever to get to the bottom, how can you get there if the guy

Kofi Annan walks with Benon Sevan, former executive director of the United Nations Office of Iraq program, in April 2003. When the Oil-for-Food scandal erupted, Annan accepted responsibility, though Sevan was later found to have engaged in "an irreconcilable conflict of interest" by choosing the companies that bought Saddam Hussein's oil.

who was in charge during the course of this fraud and corruption is the guy now who is supposed to be ferreting it out?"[66]

The brunt of the scandal did fall on Annan, who also admitted, "As chief administrative officer of the United Nations Organization, I am responsible and accountable to the member states for its management."[67] Even more alarming, Annan's son, Kojo, was somehow involved. His former employer, the Swiss company Cotecna Inspections, which had been specifically hired as a contractor for the OFF program, had made undisclosed payments to Kojo, even after he left the company in 1998.

In reality, fingers can point in many directions. Investigations proved that Annan had no knowledge of the scandal, but obviously members of his staff will be found guilty, possibly including Benon Sevan—former head of the Office of the Iraq Program. In 2003, Annan paid tribute to Sevan in a speech to the Security Council on the handover of the OFF. He praised Sevan as serving "far beyond the call of duty."[68] It would no doubt be a terrible blow to Annan if his once trusted colleague turned out to be corrupt. In January 2004, the Iraqi newspaper *Al-Mada* published a list of people and organizations, including UN personnel, who supposedly received vouchers from the Iraqi government to buy oil.

Even though America waves a fist at Annan and the UN, the United States may also have been involved. For example, the CIA report says that the bulk of illegal transactions were government-to-government deals, between Iraq and several other countries, for oil trade outside the OFF. According to the report, these deals earned Iraq $7.5 billion. The largest of these transactions was with Jordan—a country that up until the OFF program was Iraq's financial lifeline. The UN did nothing to sever ties between Iraq and Jordan, because the Security Council—of which the United States is the most influential member—had decided in May 1991 that no action should be taken to interfere with trade between the two countries. This was most likely due to the fact that Jordan is the United States' closest ally in the Middle East. Also, the maritime smuggling took place under the Multinational Interception

Force, a group of member nations that responded to the Security Council's plea to stop Iraqi smuggling. As it turned out, the force consisted almost entirely of the U.S. Navy. The supposed UN failure to intercept Hussein's tankers filled with illegal oil was actually on the watch of the U.S. Navy.

Who is responsible for the scandal is still in question, and the whole truth may never come out. Blame may be of little importance when the damage has already been done, however. After Annan gained respect for the UN with his dynamic reforms, he was now back at square one. How would he fix this mess?

The secretary-general immediately released the internal audits and flung open the doors of the UN to investigators. While awaiting the investigation's final report, Annan is focusing on issues of management and accountability in the organization. He plans to restructure management systems with stricter financial disclosures—what he refers to as transparency—to prevent anything like this from happening again.

> Transparency is the only way to deal with allegations [like those surrounding the OFF program], and by far the best way to prevent corruption from happening in the first place. That, I believe, will be one of the main lessons we have to learn from this affair, whatever the outcome of the inquiry.[69]

As the reports trickle in, Annan admits that the scandal is "deeply embarrassing to all of us." He adds, "The Inquiry Committee has ripped away the curtain, and shone a harsh light into the most unsightly corners of the Organization. None of us— Member States, Secretariat, Agencies, Funds or Programs—can be proud of what it has found."[70]

PEACE FOR AFRICA

Throughout his years in college, Annan always hoped to do something to help his home continent of Africa. While working with the United Nations, Annan tried to resolve problems in Africa whenever he was able, sometimes succeeding, sometimes not. Bringing an end to armed conflict in Africa still remains an elusive goal, but Annan is not giving up. The persistence of conflict in Africa, the secretary-general asserts, poses an ongoing challenge for the UN, because it goes to the heart of the organization's mandate: "For the United Nations there is no higher goal,

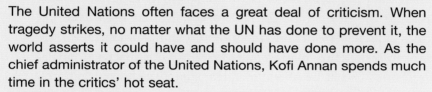

Critics of the Peacemaker

The United Nations often faces a great deal of criticism. When tragedy strikes, no matter what the UN has done to prevent it, the world asserts it could have and should have done more. As the chief administrator of the United Nations, Kofi Annan spends much time in the critics' hot seat.

Although most people around the world believed the Nobel Committee made an inspired choice with Annan, there were some who felt his work did not deserve the award. These critics often cited the atrocities of Rwanda and Bosnia, blaming Annan—the man in charge of peacekeeping—for the lack of action. Some critics assert that Annan did not push the Security Council hard enough, that he did not make enough noise to capture public attention. They claim he owns full responsibility for the horrendous genocide and violations of human rights, and these failures do not merit a reward for peace.

On the other hand, Annan is often praised for making the UN a more efficient institution and rebuilding the organization's prestige and authority in the recent years. Because of his reforms, the United Nations is prepared to play an important role in the international fight against terrorism. In Afghanistan, East Timor, and Kosovo, Annan lent an active hand in rebuilding governments and societies that can offer peace and security. His raw determination to make the world a better place for everyone, regardless of race, religion, or gender, has brought him far more respect around the globe than it has criticism.

no deeper commitment and no greater ambition than preventing armed conflict," he says.

What is necessary is an honest reexamination of the UN's experience in Africa. Instead of focusing on Africa's problems, Annan suggests the UN analyzes the political, historical, economic, and social causes of conflict. After a sober review of the failures and successes of previous peacekeeping and humanitarian missions, he can draw clear conclusions of what should be done next. Annan has tried to study the complex roots of conflict and develop plans for good and sustainable governments that will provide lasting peace.

Despite targeting the regions torn with conflict, Annan tries to instill hope. "Africa today is striving to make positive change, and in many places these efforts are beginning to bear fruit," he points out. "In the carnage and tragedy that afflicts some parts of Africa, we must not forget the bright spots or overlook the achievements."

The roots of conflict in Africa are as diverse and complex as the continent itself. Years of colonial rule brought artificial boundaries that caused divisions between ethnic groups and made national unity difficult. In some regions, such as central Africa, warring has been intensified by the competition for scarce land and water. In addition, Annan comments, despite the horror and devastation of war, "there are many who profit from chaos." These people, such as international arms merchants, actually have a profitable interest in prolonging war.

In peacemaking efforts, Annan stresses that early-warning systems are of little use without early action. Rapid diplomatic interventions are the most cost-effective way to prevent wars. In order to be quick, the United Nations needs to be prepared. Under Annan's directions, the UN has established an Executive Committee on Peace and Security, headquartered in Addis Ababa, Ethiopia, to achieve better coordination between the UN, OAU, and Africa's subregional organizations. Although sanctions can be an effective tool in peacekeeping, they can sometimes inflict serious hardships on civilians. Annan suggests UN sanctions be targeted at decision-makers and their families, such as freezing their assets and limiting their ability to travel. More important, Annan presses for the restriction of arms exports to areas of conflict. The fighting cannot continue without the tools to fight. Therefore, the UN is attempting to identify international arms merchants and monitor their activities.

Of the 32 UN peacekeeping missions launched since 1989, 13 have taken place in Africa. But memories of Somalia and Rwanda "continue to hobble the United Nations' capacity to respond swiftly and decisively to crises," the secretary-general admits. Past experiences cannot continue to hold back member states from their duty as international peacekeepers. Annan insists, "Where a peace process is needed and does not exist, it is the role of the UN, with the Organization of African Unity (OAU), to help create one." Perhaps Annan's programs will eventually bring peace and security to the homeland he is so devoted to.

Kofi Annan continues to tackle peacekeeping and humanitarian missions all over the world every day, whether it is building governments in postwar Iraq and Kosovo or securing peace in Bosnia. He is never focused on just one task, just one conflict, just one nation in need. His job of keeping the peace is greater than one man can hold, and that is why he works to motivate the nations of the world to help one another. On the personal side, Annan and Nane have discussed settling in Ghana after his retirement. He is considering opening a tomato plant there. If he decides not to, perhaps the secretary-general will fulfill his dream of becoming a farmer.

Nobel Peace Prize
Acceptance Speech: Kofi A. Annan

Today in Afghanistan, a girl will be born. Her mother will hold her and feed her, comfort her and care for her—just as any mother would anywhere in the world. In these most basic acts of human nature, humanity knows no divisions. But to be born a girl in today's Afghanistan is to begin life centuries away from the prosperity that one small part of humanity has achieved. It is to live under conditions that many of us would consider inhuman.

I speak of a girl in Afghanistan, but I might equally well have mentioned a baby boy or girl in Sierra Leone. No one today can claim ignorance of the cost that this divide imposes on the poor and dispossessed who are no less deserving of human dignity, fundamental freedoms, security, food and education than any of us. The cost, however, is not borne by them alone. Ultimately, it is born by all of us—North and South, rich and poor, men and women of all races and religions.

Today's real borders are not between nations, but between powerful and powerless, free and fettered, privileged and humiliated. Today, no walls can separate humanitarian or human rights crises in one part of the world from national security crises in another.

Scientists tell us that the world of nature is so small and interdependent that a butterfly flapping its wings in the Amazon rainforest can generate a violent storm on the other side of earth. This principle is known as the "Butterfly Effect." Today, we realize, perhaps more than ever, that the world of human activity also has its own "Butterfly Effect"—for better or for worse.

We have entered the third millennium through a gate of fire. If today, after the horror of 11 September, we see better, and we see further—we will realize that humanity is indivisible. New threats make no distinction between races, nations or regions. A new insecurity has entered every mind, regardless of wealth or status. A deeper awareness of the bonds that bind us all—in pain as in prosperity—has gripped young and old.

In the early beginnings of the 21st century—a century already violently disabused of any hopes that progress towards global peace and prosperity is inevitable—this new reality can no longer be ignored. It must be confronted.

The 20th century was perhaps the deadliest in human history, devastated by innumerable conflicts, untold suffering, and unimaginable crimes. Time after time, a group or a nation inflicted extreme violence on another, often driven by irrational hatred and suspicion, or unbounded arrogance and thirst for power and resources. In response to these cataclysms, the leaders of the world came together at mid-century to unite the nations as never before.

A forum was created—the United Nations—where all nations could join forces to affirm the dignity and worth of every person, and to secure peace and development for all peoples. Here States could unite to strengthen the rule of law, recognize and address the needs of the poor, restrain man's brutality and greed, conserve the resources and beauty of nature, sustain the equal rights of men *and* women, and provide for the safety of future generations.

We thus inherit from the 20th century the political, as well as the scientific and technological power, which—if only we have the will to use them—give us the chance to vanquish poverty, ignorance and disease.

In the 21st century I believe the mission of the United Nations will be defined by a new, more profound, awareness of the sanctity and dignity of every human life, regardless of race or religion. This will require us to look beyond the framework of States, and beneath the surface of nations or communities. We must focus, as never before, on improving the conditions of the individual men and women who give the state or nation its richness and character. We must begin with the young Afghan girl, recognizing that saving that one life is to save humanity itself.

Over the past five years, I have often recalled that the United Nations' Charter begins with the words: "We the peoples." What is not always recognized is that "we the peoples" are made up of individuals whose claims to the most fundamental rights have too often been sacrificed in the supposed interests of the state or the nation.

A genocide begins with the killing of one man—not for what he has done, but because of who he is. A campaign of "ethnic cleansing" begins with one neighbor turning on another. Poverty begins when even one child is denied his or her fundamental right to education. What begins with the failure to uphold the dignity of one life, all too often ends with a calamity for entire nations.

In this new century, we must start from the understanding that peace belongs not only to states or peoples, but to each and every member of those communities. The sovereignty of States must no longer be used as a shield for gross violations of human rights. Peace must be made real and tangible in the daily existence of every individual in need. Peace must be sought, above all, because it is the condition for every member of the human family to live a life of dignity and security.

The rights of the individual are of no less importance to immigrants and minorities in Europe and the Americas than to women in Afghanistan or children in Africa. They are as fundamental to the poor as to the rich; they are as necessary to the security of the developed world as to that of the developing world.

From this vision of the role of the United Nations in the next century flow three key priorities for the future: eradicating poverty, preventing conflict, and promoting democracy. Only in a world that is rid of poverty can all men and women make the most of their abilities. Only where individual rights are respected can differences be channelled politically and resolved peacefully. Only in a democratic environment, based on respect for diversity and dialogue, can individual self-expression and self-government be secured, and freedom of association be upheld.

Source: Kofi Annan, Nobel Lecture. Available at http://nobelprize.org/ nobel_prizes/peace/laureates/2001/annan-lecture.html. © 2001 The Nobel Foundation.

1938	**April 8** Kofi Annan is born in Kumasi, Ghana.
1947	The anticolonial group United Gold Coast Convention is formed.
1957	Annan graduates from high school; The Gold Coast, a British colony, becomes the independent nation of Ghana.
1961	Annan graduates from Macalester College in St. Paul, Minnesota, with a bachelor's degree in economics.
1961–1962	Annan does his graduate studies in economics at the Institut universitaire des hautes études internationales in Geneva, Switzerland.
1962	Joins the UN as an administrative and budget officer in the World Health Organization in Geneva.
1971–1972	As a Sloan Fellow at the Massachusetts Institute of Technology, Annan receives a Master of Science degree in management.
1974	Annan goes back to Ghana; becomes director of the Ghana Tourist Development Company.
1976	Annan returns to Geneva and the United Nations.
1980	Annan is appointed to be deputy director of administration and head of personnel in the Office of the UN High Commission for Refugees (UNHCR) in Geneva and the UN headquarters in NY.
1984	Annan and Nane Lagergren marry at the chapel in at the UN headquarters in New York.

1987 Annan is appointed as assistant secretary-general for human resources management and security coordinator for the UN system.

1991 **January 16** Annan meets with Saddam Hussein to negotiate release of hostages detained behind Iraqi lines.

1990 Annan is appointed assistant secretary-general for programme planning, budgets and finance, and controller.

1992 Annan is appointed under-secretary-general of peacekeeping; during this time, he oversees the sending of UN peacekeepers to Bosnia.

1994 **April–June** Hutu extremists in Rwanda conduct genocide of Tutsi people; during the 100-day span, approximately 800,000 Tutsi are murdered.

1997 Annan begins his first term as UN secretary-general.

2000 **April** Annan announces his eight Millennium Development Goals for the UN, outlining actions needed to end poverty and inequality, improve education, reduce the spread of HIV/AIDS, safeguard the environment, and protect all people from violence.

2001 Annan is jointly awarded the Nobel Peace Prize, with the United Nations as co-recipient.

2002 Annan's second term as UN secretary-general begins.

May 20 East Timor becomes an independent democratic republic.

2004 Oil-For-Food scandal erupts, implicating, among others, Annan's son, Kojo.

2007 **January 1** Succeeded by Ban Ki-moon as secretary-general of the United Nations.

Chapter 1

1. David Grubin, pro./dir. Kofi Annan: Center of the Storm, PBS Home Video, 2003.
2. Ibid.
3. Ibid.

Chapter 2

4. Ibid.
5. Basil Davidson, *Modern Africa: A Social and Political History,* New York: Longman, 1994, p. 139.
6. Grubin, Kofi Annan: Center of the Storm.

Chapter 3

7. Kofi Annan, Transcript of a Press Conference by the Secretary-General at the National Press Club, Washington D.C., March 12, 1998.
8. Carroll Bogert, "The Peacekeeper," Newsweek (December 23, 1996), pp. 30–31.
9. Kofi Annan, Transcript, March 12, 1998.
10. Ibid.
11. Ibid.
12. "Kofi Annan '61." Macalester College. http://www.macalester. edu/admissions/academics/ after_mac/kofi.html.
13. "Macalaster's Own," *Macalaster Today.* Available at http://www. macalaster.edu/mactoday/ summer2006/annan.html.
14. Associated Press, "Macalester Alumnus Kofi Annan Receives Nobel Peace Prize" (December 11, 2001).

15. Barbara Crossette, "UN Leader Discovered U.S., and Earmuffs, as a Student," The Socio-Path, Rice University Sociology Department, vol. 1, no.15 (January 10, 1997).
16. Ibid.
17. Ibid.
18. Basil Davidson, *Modern Africa: A Social and Political History*, New York: Longman, 1989, p. 255.

Chapter 4

19. Barbara Crossette, "How U.N. Chief Discovered U.S., and Earmuffs," *The New York Times*, (January 7, 1997).
20. Ibid.
21. Kofi Annan, interviewed by Jonathan Mann of CNN, December 10, 2001, Oslo, Norway. (Unofficial transcript: "The Secretary-General off the Cuff." UN.org. http://www.un.org/ News/ossg/sgcu1001.htm.).
22. Ibid.
23. James Traub, "Kofi Annan's Biggest Headache," *The New York Times Magazine* (April 5, 1998).

Chapter 5

24. Stanley Meisler, *United Nations: The First Fifty Years*, New York: Atlantic Monthly Press, 1995, p. 279.
25. Ibid., p. 283.
26. Ibid., p. 286.
27. Ibid., p. 287.
28. Ibid., p. 294.
29. Ibid., p. 295.

30. Ibid., p. 297.
31. Ibid.
32. Ibid., p. 305.
33. Ibid., p. 307.
34. Ibid.
35. Meisler, *United Nations: The First Fifty Years*, p. 309.
36. Grubin, *Kofi Annan: Center of the Storm*.
37. Meisler, *United Nations: The First Fifty Years*, p. 309.

Chapter 6
38. Ibid., p. 316.
39. Ibid., p. 318.
40. Ibid., p. 321.
41. Barbara Crossette, "Salesman for Unity: Kofi Atta Annan," *The New York Times*, December 14, 1996.
42. Grubin, *Kofi Annan: Center of the Storm*.

Chapter 7
43. "On the Job." PBS: Center of the Storm. http://www.pbs.org/wnet/un/life/map4.html.
44. Ibid.
45. "Life Map." PBS: Center of the Storm. http://www.pbs.org/wnet/un/life/index.html.
46. Reuters, "Annan, a Ghanaian, Moves in as the New Leader of the U.N.," *The New York Times*, January 3, 1997.
47. Ibid.
48. Kofi Annan, *Towards a Culture of Prevention*, New York: Carnegie Corporation of New York, 1999, p. 38.
49. Ibid., p. 3.

50. "What Are the Millennium Development Goals?" UN.org. http://www.un.org/millenniumgoals/index.html.
51. Lally Weymouth, "Giving Saddam One More Chance," *Newsweek* (March 9, 1998), p. 32.
52. Ibid.
53. Ibid.
54. Louise Branson and Dusko Doder, *Milosevic: Portrait of a Tyrant*. New York: The Free Press, 1999.
55. Grubin, *Kofi Annan: Center of the Storm*.

Chapter 8
56. Ibid.
57. Kofi Annan, "We the Peoples: The Role of the United Nations in the 21st Century," New York: The Nobel Foundation, 2001, p. 27.
58. Ibid., p. 29.
59. Ibid., p. 39.
60. UN News Service. "Nobel Award Should 'Urge Us Forward,' Secretary-General Tells Staff." UN.org. October 12, 2001. http://www.un.org/apps/news/storyAr.asp?NewsID=1794&Cr=Nobel&Cr1=Prize.
61. Ibid.
62. Grubin, *Kofi Annan: Center of the Storm*.

Chapter 9
63. Ibid.
64. Ibid.

65. Ibid.

66. Brian Ross and Rhonda Schwartz, "Americans' Role Eyed in U.N. Oil Scandal: Were American Oil Brokers Involved in Iraq Oil Kickback Schemes?" ABC News Internet Ventures. December 1, 2004.

67. Kofi Annan, The secretary-general's statement on the Interim Report of the Independent Inquiry Committee into the Oil-for-Food program, read by his Chef de Cabinet, Mark Malloch Brown at a press conference in New York on February 3, 2005. Available on the United Nations Web site.

68. Kofi Annan, The Secretary-General's statement to the Security Council on the closure of the Oil-for-Food in New York, November 20, 2003. Available at http://www.un.org.

69. "The United Nations Oil-for-Food Programme." UN.org. http://www.un.org/News/dh/iraq/oip/facts-oilforfood.htm.

70. Kofi Annan, The secretary-general's statement to the Security Council on receipt of the Independent Inquiry Committee (IIC) Report on Oil-for Food in New York, September 7, 2005.

BIBLIOGRAPHY

Annan, Kofi. *Towards a Culture of Prevention: Statements by the Secretary-General of the United Nations.* New York: Carnegie Commission on Preventing Deadly Conflict, December 1999.

Basic Facts About the United Nations. New York: United Nations, 2000.

Bell, P.M.H. *The World Since 1945: An International History.* New York: Oxford University Press, 2001.

Burgess, Stephen. *The United Nations Under Bourtros Boutros-Ghali, 1992–1997.* Lanham, Md.: Scarecrow Press, 2001.

Crossette, Barbara. "How UN Chief Discovered U.S., and Ear-muffs." *The New York Times* (January 7, 1997).

"Salesman for Unity: Kofi Annan." *The New York Times* (December 14, 1996).

David, Basil. *Modern Africa: A Social and Political History.* New York: Longman, 1994.

Editorial Desk, *New York Times.* "Kofi Annan's Nobel Prize." *The New York Times* (October 14, 2001).

Emmerij, Louis. *Ahead of the Curve?: UN Ideas and Global Challenges.* Bloomington: Indiana University Press, 2001.

The Encyclopedia of World History: Ancient, Medieval, and Modern, Chronologically Arranged. Boston: Houghton Mifflin, 2001.

Goldberg, Beryl. "An Interview With Kofi Annan." *Encyclopedia Britannica*, September 2001.

Gordon, Joy. "UN Oil for Food 'Scandal'." *The Nation* (December 6, 2004).

Grubin, David, dir. *Kofi Annan: Center of the Storm.* PBS Home Video, 2003.

Harrelson, Max. *Fires All Around the Horizon: The UN's Uphill Battle to Preserve the Peace.* New York: Praeger, 1989.

McWilliams, Wayne C., and Harry Piotrowski. *The World Since 1945: A History of International Relations*. Boulder, Colo.: Lynne Rienner, 2001.

Meisler, Stanley. *United Nations: The First Fifty Years*. New York: Atlantic Monthly Press, 1995.

Myers, Steven Lee. "Administration Proposes Paying UN Debt, but Congress Resists." *The New York Times* (December 30, 1996).

"Kofi Annan, Center of the Storm." PBS Online. Available at http://www.pbs.org/wnet/un/index.html.

"1994: Rwanda, 1995: Srebrenica—2001: Nobel Peace Prize to Kofi Annan?" Petitiononline.com. Available at http://www.petitiononline.com/annan/petition.html.

Reuters. "Annan, a Ghanaian, Moves in as the New Leader of the UN." *The New York Times* (January 3, 1997).

Rosenthal, Andrew. "Confrontation in the Gulf; Baghdad Warns Diplomats Against 'Act of Aggression'; Hussein Shows Off Hostages." *The New York Times* (August 24, 1990).

Ross, Brian, and Rhonda Schwartz. "Americas' Role Eyed in UN Oil Scandal: Were American Oil Brokers Involved in Iraq Oil Kickback Schemes?" *ABCNews*. Available at http://abcnews.go.com/WNT/print?id=295926. December 1, 2004.

Saul, Mahir. *West African Challenge to the Empire: Culture and History in the Volta-Bani Anticolonial War*. Athens, Ohio: Ohio University Press, 2001.

"Transcript of Press Conference by Secretary-General Kofi Annan at the National Press Club, Washington D.C.," *Science Blog*. Available at http://www.scienceblog.com/community/older/archives/L/1998/A/un980266.html. March 12, 1998.

Traub, James. "Kofi Annan's Biggest Headache." *New York Times Magazine* (April 5, 1998).

UN High Commissioner for Refugees. *The State of the World's Refugees, 2000: Fifty Years of Humanitarian Action.* Geneva: UNCHR; New York: Oxford University Press, 2000.

Urquhart, Sir Brian. "Peacekeeping: We Need Serious Rethinking." *United Nations Chronicle*, Online Edition, vol. XXXV, no. 3 (1998), Department of Public Information.

Vinocur, John. "Nobel Peace Award Goes to the UN Agency for Its Refugee Work." *The New York Times* (October 15, 1981).

Weymouth, Lally. "Giving Saddam One More Chance: Annan on His Last-minute Agreement With Iraq." *Newsweek* (March 9, 1998): p. 32.

World History: Comprehensive Volume. Belmont, Calif.: Wadsworth/Thomson Learning, 2002.

Annan, Kofi. *Towards a Culture of Prevention: Statements by the Secretary-General of the United Nations.* New York: Carnegie Commission on Preventing Deadly Conflict, December 1999.

Basic Facts About the United Nations. New York: United Nations, 2000.

Burgess, Stephen. *The United Nations Under Bourtros Boutros-Ghali, 1992–1997.* Lanham, Md.: Scarecrow Press, 2001.

Emmerij, Louis. *Ahead of the Curve?: UN Ideas and Global Challenges.* Bloomington: Indiana University Press, 2001.

Harrelson, Max. *Fires All Around the Horizon: The UN's Uphill Battle to Preserve the Peace.* New York: Praeger, 1989.

Kofi Annan: Center of the Storm. PBS Home Video, 2003.

Meisler, Stanley. *United Nations: The First Fifty Years.* New York: Atlantic Monthly Press, 1995.

PICTURE CREDITS

117

RACHEL A. KOESTLER-GRACK has worked with nonfiction books as an editor and writer since 1999. She has covered historical topics, such as the colonial era, the Civil War era, the Great Depression, the civil rights movement, and has written numerous historical biographies.